WOLE SOYINKA

MPALIVE-HANGSON MSISKA

Northcote House
in association with the
British Council

© Copyright 1998 by Mpalive-Hangson Msiska

First published in 1998 by Northcote House Publishers Ltd, Plymbridge House, Estover Road, Plymouth PL6 7PY, United Kingdom.
Tel: +44 (01752) 202368 Fax: +44 (01752) 202330.

All rights reserved. No part of this work may be reproduced or stored in an information retrieval system (other than short extracts for the purposes of review) without the express permission of the Publishers given in writing.

British Library Cataloguing-in-Publication Data
A catalogue record for this book is available from the British Library

ISBN 0-7463-0811-6

Typeset by PDQ Typesetting, Newcastle-under-Lyme
Printed and bound in the United Kingdom

10034 33937

To Mupa Shumba for his Ogunian example

Contents

Acknowledgements

I owe a debt of gratitude to a number of friends for moral and other forms of support during the writing of the book, in particular John Kraniauskas, Davis Gazi, Vicky Davies, Jose Unamuno, Yoliswa Siyolwe, Susan Forster, Jack Mapanje, Rosemary Weeks, Pat Mhone, Wangui wa Goro, Sam Chibambo, Eda Colbert, and James Gibbs, especially for sharing his enthusiasm for Soyinka when he was my tutor at the University of Malawi and helping to bring Soyinka's work to life with the University Travelling Theatre, and to Anthony Nazombe for his incomparable Eman in *The Strong Breed*. I am thankful to Femi Abodunrin for a passionate discussion of Soyinka and Yoruba culture on his way to Malawi. I thrive on the love and support of my extended family, among whom on this occasion I would like to thank: Emily, Emily Kachipeya, Dairess-Dominique, Ndinda, Yoram, Mestina, Regina, Kingston, Hudson and Hilary, my mother and father. Thanks are also due to colleagues in the English Department at Birkbeck College, especially to the Research Committee which gave me the time and resources to complete the book. I am equally indebted to Anthony Downey who was a superb research assistant.

I should also thank Wole Soyinka for the gift of his work and his publishers, particularly, Oxford and Cambridge University Presses, Methuen, Rex Collings, Heinemann, Minerva, Vintage, New Horn, and Spectrum Books for permission to quote from his work.

Most especially, I would like to thank Isobel Armstrong for giving me this opportunity to engage with my favourite author, and also for her constant encouragement.

Biographical Outline*

1934   Born in Abeokuta, Western Nigeria.

1938–45   Pupil at St Peter's School, Abeokuta, and Abeokuta Grammar School.

1946–50   Secondary school student at Government College, Ibadan.

1952–4   Student at the University College Ibadan, now University of Ibadan. Founds the Pyrates, a confraternity.

1954–7   Completes a BA (Hons.) degree in English at Leeds University and contributes regularly to the British Broadcasting Corporation.

1957–60   Script reader for the Royal Court Theatre, London. *The Invention*, as well as excerpts from *A Dance of the African Forests* performed at the theatre. Poems included in Langston Hughes' *African Treasury*. Returns to Nigeria and forms the 1960 Masks Drama Company. Directs *A Dance of the Forests* for the independence celebrations of Nigeria: the play wins the Encounter Award.

1961–3   Rockefeller Research Fellow in Drama at the University of Ibadan. Excerpts from *The House of Abenigeji* (a play) included in Frances Ademola's *Reflections*. Lecturer in English at the University of Ife. *The Lion and the Jewel* and *A Dance of the Forests* (plays) published. Poems included in Gerald Moore and Ulli Beier (eds.), *The Penguin Modern Poetry from Africa*.

1964   Founds Orisun Theatre. *The Strong Breed* (a play) televised in the United States. *The Strong Breed* and *The Trials of Brother Jero* (a play) staged at Greenwich Mews Theatre, New York. *Five Plays* published.

1965   *Before the Blackout* (a satirical revue) produced in Lagos and Ibadan, Nigeria, and *The Road* directed by David Thompson at the Theatre Royal, Stratford, London.

	Arrested and acquitted on a charge of armed robbery of a cassette tape during a pirate radio denunciation of election results broadcast on the Nigerian Broadcasting Corporation. *The Road* and *The Interpreters* published. Directs *Kongi's Harvest* in Lagos and is appointed Senior Lecturer in English and Acting Head of Department, University of Lagos.
1966–7	*Kongi's Harvest* performed at the Festival of Negro Arts in Senegal and *The Trials of Brother Jero* (Hampstead Theatre) and *The Lion and the Jewel* (the Royal Court Theatre), London. *Kongi's Harvest* and *Idanre and Other Poems* published. Joint winner of the John Whiting Drama prize with Tom Stoppard, and appointed Head of Department of Theatre Arts, Ibadan. Arrested by the Federal Military Government for contacts with secessionist Biafra and for campaigning against the supply of arms to both sides.
1968	Awarded the Jock Campbell *New Statesman* Literary Award. *The Forest of a Thousand Demons* (translation of D. O. Fagunwa's novel, *Ogboju Ode Ninu Igbo Irunmale*) published.
1969	*Three Short Plays* published. Released from detention and returns to his post at Ibadan. Directs *Kongi's Harvest* at Ife and Ibadan.
1970–1	Directs an early version of *Madmen and Specialists* at the Eugene O'Neill Theatre Centre, Waterford and Harlem, USA, and the complete version in Ibadan and Ife. *Before the Blackout* published. Directs Pirandello's *The Jar*, Wale Ogunyemi's *Eshu Elegbara*, and Ben Caldwell's *The Fanatic*, Ibadan.
1972	*The Man Died* and *Shuttle in the Crypt* published.
1973–4	Visiting Fellow, Churchill College, Cambridge. *Season of Anomy* and *Collected Plays I* published. The National Theatre performs *The Bacchae of Euripides* at the Old Vic, London.
1974–5	*Poems from Black Africa* published. Editor of *Transition (Ch'Indaba)* (a journal), and Visiting Professor, University of Ghana, Legon. Secretary-General of the Union of Writers of the African Peoples. *Collected Plays II* published. *The Detainee* (a radio play) broadcast on the BBC World Service.

1976   *Myth, Literature and the African World* and *Ogun Abibiman* (a long poem) published. Appointed Professor of Comparative Literature at Ife, where he directs *Death and the King's Horseman.*

1977   Advocates the adoption of Swahili as the lingua franca for Africa at the Lagos Festac (The International Festival of Negro Arts and Culture) and also produces *Opera Wonyosi*, Ife. Helps set up the Oyo State Road Safety Corps.

1978   Head of Department of Dramatic Arts, University of Ife. Creates Unife Guerrilla Theatre, performing satirical revues.

1979–80   Visiting Professor, Yale University. Directs *Death and the King's Horseman* at the Goodman Theatre, Chicago and the J. F. Kennedy Center, Washington and also *Rice Unlimited* (satirical review) at Ibadan and Ife. Chairman of the Oyo State Road Safety Corps.

1981–2   *Ake: The Years of Childhood, Opera Wonyosi, A Play of Giants,* and *The Critic and Society: Barthes, Leftocracy and Other Mythologies* (inaugural lecture) published. Lectures on 'Shakespeare and the Living Dramatist' at Stratford-on-Avon, England. *Die Still Dr Godspeak* broadcast on BBC World Service. Tours Nigeria with *Priority Projects* (satirical revue).

1983–4   Directs *Requiem for a Futurologist* at Ife and *The Road* at the Goodman Theatre, Chicago. Releases an album of political songs, *Unlimited Liability Company. Six Plays* published.

1985   *Requiem for a Futorulogist* published. Retires from the University of Ife.

1986   Awarded the Nobel Prize for Literature and made Commander of the Federal Republic of Nigeria (CFR).

1987–8   *Art, Dialogue and Outrage* (essays) and *Childe Internationale* (a play) published. Road Commissioner, Federal Road Safety Commission.

1989–90   *Mandela's Earth and Other Poems* and *Isara: A Voyage around Essay* (biography) published. Death threat after publishing article in support of Salman Rushdie: 'Jihad for Freedom', *The African Guardian*, 2 Feb. 1989. 'Spiking the Wall': lecture at the Institute of Contemporary Arts, London.

1991–2   *The Credo of Being and Nothingness* (essay) and *From Zia, with Love* and *A Scourge of Hyacinths* (plays) published.
1993–4   Exile in Europe and America. *Ibadan: The Penkelemes Years – A Memoir, 1946–1965* published.
1995–7   *The Beatification of Area Boy: A Lagosian Kaleidoscope* (a play) published and staged at West Yorkshire Playhouse as part of Africa 95 Festival. *The Open Sore of a Continent: A Personal Narrative of the Nigerian Crisis* published. Campaigns against the military dictatorship in Nigeria and is consequently sentenced to death *in absentia*. Visiting Professor, Harvard University.
1998   Woodruff Professor of the Arts, Emory University, Atlanta.

* The outline is based on James Gibbs's biographical work, especially his *Soyinka* (London, 1986); and the outline in the introduction to *Soyinka: Six Plays* (London, 1984).

Abbreviations and References

For most of the plays, I have used the versions in *Soyinka: Collected Plays 1 and 2* (Oxford: 1973 and 1974), referred to as *SCP 1 and 2* respectively throughout the book; for *Camwood on the Leaves, Death and the King's Horseman*, and *Opera Wonyosi* I have used those in *Soykinka: Six Plays* (London: Methuen, 1984) shortened to *SSP* in the book.

Abbreviations for single plays and other primary texts quoted are as follows:

A.	*Ake: The Years of Childhood*
ADO	*Art, Dialogue and Outrage* (essays)
BAB	*The Beatification of Area Boy: A Lagosian Kaleidoscope*
CBN	*The Credo of Being and Nothingness*
Gates	Henry Louis Gates et al (eds), *Black American Literature Forum*
Gibbs 1	James Gibbs and Bernth Lindfors (eds), *Research on Wole Soyinka*
Gibbs 2	James Gibbs, *Soyinka: Critical Perspective*
I.	*The Intepreters*
IOP	*Idanre and Other Poems*
IP	*Ibadan: The Penkelemes Years – A Memoir, 1946–1965*
IS	*Isara: A Voyage around Essay*
Maja-Pearce	Adewale Maja-Pearce (ed), *Wole Soyinka: An Appraisal*
MD	*The Man Died: Prison Notes*
MEOP	*Mandela's Earth and Other Poems*
MLA	*Myth, Literature and the African World*
Moore	Gerald Moore et al (eds), *Modern Poetry from Africa*
OA	*Ogun Abibiman* (a long poem)
OSC	*The Open Sore of a Continent: A Personal Narrative of*

	the Nigerian Crisis
PG	*A Play of Giants*
SA	*Season of Anomy*
SC	*A Shuttle in the Crypt*
SCP 1	*Soyinka: Collected Plays 1*
SCP 2	*Soyinka: Collected Plays 2*
SSP	*Soyinka: Six Plays*
St John's	St John's Gospel in *The Holy Bible, King James Version*

1

Introduction

Wole Soyinka was awarded the 1986 Nobel Prize for Literature in obvious acknowledgement of his international stature as a writer and also of his lifelong commitment to the cause of justice – for him, writing is inextricably linked with the effort to create a just and democratic society in post-colonial Africa. Soyinka's use of literature and the theatre in the service of humanity has a long history. For instance, his earliest appearance as an actor on the London stage at the Royal Court Theatre in 1958 was in *Eleven Men Dead at Hola*, a revue critical of British colonial policy in Kenya where some Mau-Mau detainees had been beaten to death by camp officers. The following year, his play *The Invention*, which condemned Apartheid in South Africa, was performed at the same theatre. It is a mark of exceptional ethical consistency, though not particularly pleasant for the writer himself, that in the 1990s he is in political exile, this time protesting against the violation of human rights by a post-colonial military dictatorship in his native Nigeria whose atrocities include the execution of the writer Ken Saro Wiwa.

Even so, Soyinka is evidently the pride of the Nigerian nation: for example, soon after getting the Nobel Prize he was made Knight Commander of the Federal Republic of Nigeria, an honour reserved for exceptional service to the country. Although this gesture of national recognition may have given Soyinka great personal satisfaction, the irony of it would most certainly not have escaped him. A large part of his creative achievement is devoted to the castigation of post-colonial leadership, especially in Nigeria, and General Ibrahim Babangida, the head of state who had him knighted, was himself not so markedly different from Soyinka's usual military strongman. Thus, despite being highly regarded by Nigerian officialdom,

Soyinka has always been a thorn in the flesh of successive governments ever since the time in 1965 when, following rigged regional elections, a man allegedly resembling him made a pirate radio broadcast on the national broadcasting network denouncing the results. Acquitted on a legal technicality in this instance, Soyinka was later imprisoned without trial during the 1967–70 Nigerian civil war for his effort to get the supply of arms to both sides in the conflict stopped. Yet the recognition he received at home following the Nobel award must also be seen in the context of his general standing on the African continent as a whole where he is widely regarded as a leader. He is thus a prophet with honour not only in his village, but also in villages and cities miles away from his own. Where did it all start?

Olewole Akinwande Soyinka was born in 1934 in Abeokuta, Western Nigeria to a family of village school teachers. As recounted in his autobiographies, *Ake* (1981) and *Isara* (1990), Soyinka was brought up in a culturally diverse extended family in which the tension between tradition and modernity was played out daily in the lives of his parents and grandparents, all of whom were similarly caught up in the maelstrom of cultural change.[1] This tension would later characterize Soyinka's secondary and university education, especially since his formative years were mostly spent under the period of British colonial rule which put a great premium on the immersion of the 'native' in British culture. However, as Soyinka himself observes, one can exaggerate the extent of British cultural production of colonized subjectivity: his upbringing still provided significant access to the culture and traditions of his people and, indeed, it was this early exposure to the fundamentals of Yoruba culture that would later stand him in good stead in his writing career, giving him a contact with Yoruba cosmology that was deeper than would ordinarily be expected of someone brought up in a predominantly Christian and Westernized environment.

His days at the University of Ibadan saw Soyinka being introduced to aspects of European intellectual and artistic traditions, including Greek drama, to which he would return time and again for a source of style and, so it could also be said, of a *sujet* (plot) for his syncretic representation of oppression and possible redemption. His editorship of the student

2

magazine *The Eagle* gave him the perfect opportunity to practise writing and to try out some of his early political ideas. Most memorable, though, is his forming of a confraternity known as the 'Pyrates', modelled on tales of pirates the author and his colleagues had heard or read. His *nom piratical du guerre*, so to speak, was Captain Blood. This is clearly not an example of a properly colonized young 'native'; if anything it dramatizes what was to characterize Soyinka's adult life, the instinctive rebelliousness and anti-Establishment attitude which have made it difficult for him to be uncontroversial even at a time in his life when many of his colleagues have justifiably reduced their active political involvement.

It may have been this propensity in Soyinka's personality that drew him to some of the most inspiring, but patently eccentric teachers at Leeds University in the late fifties. Evidently, his encounter with G. Wilson Knight, the great Shakespearean scholar, has left an indelible mark on his work, as it was through him that Soyinka first became interested in theorizing the link between ritual and tragedy which is central to his dramaturgy. Similarly Arnold Kettle, one of the leading Marxist critics of his time, exposed the young Soyinka to the central role of class relations in political and economic formation, another recurrent theme in the author's work. Leeds was for Soyinka an opportunity not only for intellectual development, seen amply in his keenness to grapple with new ideas as well as in his active interest in student politics and literary life, but also for particularly sharpening further his creative writing skills. It is reported that he wrote profusely, broadcasting his work on BBC radio and also publishing some of it in student magazines. Significantly, the broadcasts did much to establish him back home as a serious upcoming writer and critic.[2]

However important these influences were, it is primarily Soyinka's direct experience of the theatre, in all its variety – as script writer, actor, and director – which began in earnest at the Royal Court in 1958 and which has continued throughout his life, that has profoundly shaped his writing. Additionally, one of the most invaluable experiences for the author must have been the period in the early sixties when he conducted research into traditional African drama as a Rockefeller Research Fellow at the University of Ibadan. This enabled him to travel the length and breadth of Nigeria as well as to neighbouring countries to experience at first hand, but with the benefit of a scholar's trained eye, a variety of traditional performance theatre, which provided him with a rich resource for both his creative and theoretical work, giving his pronouncements on traditional African theatre an authority greater than that derived from the mere fact of the critic having been brought up in the culture he is interpreting.

Equally important has been his work as an international academic which has resulted in Soyinka being unusually conversant with new currents in international literary criticism and the theatre, as exemplified by his masterful familiarity with the work of Roland Barthes in his critique of African Marxism at a time when Barthes may not have been the most familiar name in the African academy.[3] Generally, Soyinka's voice is that of a well-travelled cosmopolitan, as much at home in the cultural capitals of Africa as those of the Western metropole. Even more pertinently illustrative of this internationalism, if one may call it this, is his passionate and constant retracing of the African diaspora; his interest in the cultures of Cuba, of Brazil, of the Caribbean in general as well as those of African-America.

In determining Soyinka's place in African literature it may be useful to offer, cursory as it might be, a comparison with some of his fellow eminent colleagues. It needs to be noted, for example, that he does not practise the realism of detailed and historical representation seen in the work of his compatriot, Chinua Achebe; neither does he engage with questions of class in the unfettered revolutionary manner of Kenya's Ngugi wa Thiong'o. He is certainly not a Buchi Emecheta when it comes to the politics of gender.

Soyinka's politics has the forthrightness of a Ngugi wa Thiong'o without the latter's obvious ideological partisanship; it has the moral authority of Achebe, but without what the poet Odia Ofeimun describes as the 'patriarchal teacher' of Achebe's work.[4] He celebrates women's social and political power, but in ways that some feminists find modulating between absolute idealization and demonization. To his sombre voice of a Derek Walcott Soyinka adds a mischievous delight in the comic and satirical, making him perhaps the unsurpassed master of humour on the continent. His brand of satire is also reminiscent of, among others, Jonathan Swift and Alexander Pope, whom he acknowledges as being among his influences.

Politically he remains a liberal democrat with a strong Marxist revolutionary bent, making him a bit difficult to pin down at times. Whatever he is and is not, he remains a relentless campaigner for human rights and a strong opponent of all manner of dictatorship, including religious fundamentalism, both Christian and Moslem.[5] Furthermore, Soyinka has left the world of his Anglican upbringing behind, as his last reported public religious activity was leading an 'animist' gathering of students and staff at a Nigerian university.

Soyinka's assertion of traditional African religion may be seen as yet another of his grand theatrical gestures, however, while it might be that in part, it evidently emanates from a deep veneration of his Yoruba culture and a strong conviction that its world view offers a valid and adequate ground of metaphysical location for the Yoruba subject. In his programmatic statement, 'The Fourth Stage', he reconstitutes one of the Yoruba creation myths into a foundational metaphysics of his creative and critical practice. He recounts how, in the beginning, humanity and the gods were separated by an impassable chasm. Ogun, the god of iron, cut across the gulf and safely emerged on the other side, reuniting humankind and the gods. Human beings were so impressed by Ogun's heroic feat that they offered him a kingship, but at first he declined the offer, acceding to the request, however, when he could no longer bear the pressure put on him. During his reign he led humanity into a number of successful military campaigns against troublesome neighbours. Unusually, during the celebration of a particular victory, the palm wine went to his head and he turned on his army and wholly wiped it out.

Ogun's character and journey function as both metaphorical and metonymic of the structure of human experience as well as subjectivity. However, Soyinka's eclecticism does not allow for the recuperation of the mythological text as an embodiment of a pure national origin – he plays Ogun against Greek gods such as Zeus and Dionysos. It is also observable that Soyinka's Greek deities are themselves but faint copies of the originals, since they are refracted through Friedrich Nietzsche's kaleidoscopic prism of classical tragedy. It is this cultural hybridity that

5

informs Soyinka's reading of the passage of transition as well as the duality of Ogunian contradictory subjectivity: his emancipatory as well as destructive agency, and also his double tragic import within at once overlapping and separate Yoruba and Hellenic languages of tragedy. He regards duality as the fundamental structure of human experience, saying: 'the "antinomies" in my writings. But are these not a reflection of the human condition?' (*SSP* xvii–xviii) Soyinka's concept of antinomy, though, resembles less the structuralist notion of binary opposition and more the post-structuralist emphasis on textual aporia we see in Jacques Derrida or Homi Bhabha, for example.[6] For Derrida, the essential meaning of a particular assertion is always deferred because of a mediating negation inhabiting its very centre. As for Bhabha, the *third space*, the *time lag*, or the *in-between-space* undermine the will to the absolutism of difference that, according to Edward Said, structures Orientalist discourse and which Abdul JanMohamed regards as constituting the Manichean dichotomy at work in the colonial representation of Africa.[7]

Soyinka's privileging of difference has come under severe criticism from some critics who have accused him of failing to make a stand when the ideological trajectory of his work required him to do so, and it is remarkable that Derrida and Bhabha have also been accused of similar political irresponsibility.[8] This is not the only weakness that Soyinka's critics have identified in his work. It has been argued, for instance, by Chinweizu and his colleagues in their *Toward the Decolonization of African Literature* (1980), that underlying Soyinka's whole project is in fact a certain Eurocentric universalism.

This study does not aim to engage with all the criticism levelled against Soyinka, but what it hopes to demonstrate is that the writer's interest in the duality of subjectivity and social formation does not necessarily lead to ideological indeterminacy, nor can it legitimately be regarded as a symptom of an uncritical Westphilia. He offers clear resolutions to the conflicts he sets up between opposing forces, but when he does so he aims to eschew offering easy dogma and the expected settled position. Certainly, those who like their ideological positions simply validated by literature will find Soyinka irritating, as his work usually attempts to provoke in a manner reminiscent of

Bertolt Brecht's. Unlike Brecht, though, whose devices of estrangement were ultimately a means to the specific ideological end of Socialist political education, for Soyinka there are no sacred cows. His is a critique committed to a rigorous, but strategic interrogation of all forms of ideology and ideological practices, including those he himself openly subscribes to, such as Marxism and Afrocentricity. Yet, in Soyinka's view, the adoption of such a self-reflexive critical project and the admission of instances and sites of aporetic activity in every articulation of absolute difference should not be regarded as a logical pathway to a paralysing *différence* of meaning or political positioning. Perhaps the South African writer Nadine Gordimer best sums up Soyinka's creative and political practice when she describes him as a 'Blakean Tiger, whose eyes burn through the night of prejudiced indifference; no need to proclaim himself in any other way'(Maja-Pearce 39).

In case the reference to Blake is seen as a confirmation of Soyinka's alleged cultural alienation by the Chinweizu school of thought, one must hasten to clarify matters and add that Gordimer is surely suggesting that Soyinka is an African Blakean tiger! All the same, African or Blakean, for Soyinka 'a Tiger does not proclaim his tigritude, he pounces' (Gates 557).

2

Satirical Revelations

Satire is one of the two principal ways by which Soyinka, as it were, pounces on the various issues with which he engages. His work easily divides into comedy and tragedy, with the latter including texts which are serious in mood, but which do not wholly conform to any conventional meaning of the term.[1] Bernth Lindfors' use of the term 'range' in his description of Soyinka's work is suggestive of the idea of a continuum which, in my view, best describes the distribution of the satiric and the tragic within the writer's work, attesting to his desire to operate within received generic categories whilst simultaneously making them bear the distinctive multi-faceted character of his dual inhabitation of African and Western traditions. Thus, in Soyinka's creative practice, generic identity is subjected to the same logic of transformation as that evident in his representation of subject-identity, as it is brought to the moment where the law of order itself is exposed to the modifying force of disorder – what Niyi Osundare so aptly refers to as Soyinka's 'near-Messianic passion to re-create, to remake' things,' (Maja-Pearce 86) with a view to revealing what the writer himself in *Opera Wonyosi* describes as 'the maggot-infested underside of the compost heap' (*SSP* 300) of post-colonial power.

Opera Wonyosi, first produced in the late seventies, was very much the culmination of a distinctive satirical style that had evolved over a long writing career. It is visible in Soyinka's Ibadan undergraduate days, most spectacularly in the performance he and his fellow members of the Pyrates Confraternity put on during their public outing, which included colourful dress as well as singing in a style presumed typical of real pirates.[2] This strain of hyperbole finds its early written expression in Soyinka's 1950s mini-travelogues about Europe. In a 1955 letter to the editor of the University of Ibadan student magazine, *The Eagle*, Soyinka's piratical bravado of old is very much in evidence, as indicated by the following excerpt:

> I'm sure you must be hoping that I'm dead... You ought to know I'm pretty hard to kill... Why, only yesterday a car bumped into me and had to be taken to the scrap iron-dealer, while I walked home with no worse damage than some engine-oil on my trousers. (Gibbs 38)

The tongue-in-cheek self-inflation and the general sense of exaggeration in many ways give the author the freedom to exercise an unfettered outlandishness in his early narratives. For instance, in the same letter, he recounts an incident when a friend trying to greet him at a bus-stop had his hand bent backwards by gale force winds so that he ended up shaking hands with a person behind him.[3] Here Soyinka uses humour to confer on England a sort of violent exoticism that is not quite what his colleagues at the University of Ibadan, reading Shakespeare, Keats, and so on would have had in mind. This suggests that even at this early stage in his career, Soyinka is already undermining some of the dominant narratives about the metropole which formed part of the official British colonial self-representation in the colonies as well as of the imaginary of the successfully interpellated colonized subjects.

It is noteworthy that in one of Soyinka's Johnny-just-come-to-town stories excavated by James Gibbs from the BBC archives, the hero's ignorance about British culture and especially about modern technological gadgets, is a subject of much comic laughter among his hosts as well as his countrymen.[4] In one story he screams at the top of his voice, 'The stairs are sinking,' (Gibbs 1 38) when the escalator flattens out when it reaches the end, much to the embarrassment of his city-wise compatriot.

Soyinka is here operating within a universal genre typical of the first phases of modernization in which, unproblematically, the country is represented as backward and the town as civilized. Some literary examples that may have formed his background to the subject are the eighteenth-century English conduct books, and also some African-language literature written under the sponsorship of mission presses.[5] Usually, the person from the country is represented as gullible and also incapable of opposing the hierarchical structure in which he or she is inserted and judged. On the contrary, that is not the case with Soyinka's Johnny, who makes certain that whenever the English ridicule his unfamiliarity with modern gadgets he retorts by asking if any of them had ever seen a palm tree in their lives, which seems to bring about the same sort of effect on them as their ridicule does on him.[6] The efficacy of Johnny's retort is nevertheless doubtful, given that the mention of palm trees may simply conjure the world of Friday in Defoe's *Robinson Crusoe* or similar narratives in which the palm tree signifies a plenitude of Noble Savagery, but a savagery of sorts all the same. The joke about the palm tree also makes the story historically specific: one wonders whether it is still as exotic to the average British person as it was in the fifties when Soyinka wrote the stories. Be that as it may, such historical particularities do not blunt the overall satirical quality of the exchange, since the character derives great relief from his ability, not perhaps to write back to the empire, but to laugh back at it.

The protagonist's reply neatly falls within the post-colonial project of writing back to the centre, seen by the authors of *The Empire Writes Back* (1989), among others, as principally engaged in the interrogation and problematization of the colonial representation of the colonized. Yet, characteristically, Soyinka's form of writing back involves a comic dismemberment of the self as well, a trait which some African critics have condemned as undermining the construction and propagation of a radical discourse of African cultural authenticity.[7] However, as Soyinka himself has argued, such criticism shows a misunderstanding of the overall ideological function of his satirical style, for his irreverence is not an abandonment of ideological and ethical commitment, but rather a means of conducting a more demanding analysis of the surface presentation of ideas and beliefs so as to engender a deeper apprehension and consequent implementation of those values which truly promote social and political justice.

The use of satire as a means of conducting an ethical and political critique of a given ideology is amply observable in Soyinka's comic treatment of British landlords and landladies in the work written while in England. It is reported, for example, that in his unpublished play *The Invention*, he has an association of British landladies and landlords sending a donation to the

South African National Party to congratulate them on their policy of apartheid. Soyinka's resentment of landladies and landlords is a direct response to the difficulties he had in finding digs when he was an undergraduate student at Leeds.[8]

He broaches the subject satirically in his much-anthologized poem, 'Telephone conversation', which, having been part of his début programme at the Royal Court in 1959, served as one of the early markers of his particular style of wit, irony, and satire.[9] As the student's accent, similar to Soyinka's youthful English pronunciation, does not give away his racial or cultural identity, he warns the prospective landlady that he is an African.[10] As shown in the following lines, this declaration leads to a hilarious but revealing exchange on racial identity:

> The price seemed reasonable, location
> Indifferent. The landlady swore she lived
> off premises. Nothing remained
> But self-confession. 'Madam,' I warned,
> 'I hate a wasted journey – I am African.'
> Silence. Silenced transmission of
> Pressurized good-breeding... Caught I was, foully.
> 'HOW DARK?'... I had not misheard... 'ARE YOU LIGHT
> OR VERY DARK?'

(Moore 111)

It is the calmness and deadpan manner with which the persona moves from talking about the practical details of price and house location to the question of race that offers the first indication of the bitter satirical content and context of the narrative poem. It questions the language of racial categorization whose obsessive preoccupation with infinite precision seems to be an obvious exhibition of anxiety over the untenability of the ideal it is meant to represent and safeguard. Also relevant here is the fact that at the time Soyinka was working on the poem he was also extremely involved in opposing and writing about South African apartheid, something that may have impinged directly on the poem, especially in its focus not just on broad racial difference, but on the minutiae of racial divisions such as expounded and implemented in Apartheid South Africa. Furthermore, linking South Africa and Britain on the issue of race suggests that Soyinka does not regard apartheid as an isolated phenomenon, but rather as merely another site of repetition and elaboration of the prioritization of race as the domain of significant and exclusionary difference in the post-Columbus 'contact zones'.[11] This also fits in with his general sensitivity to race in his politics of decolonization most evident in his participation in the 1959 performance of the anti-racist revue *Eleven Men Dead at Hola*.

Soyinka's allusion to the wider historical context of colonial racism is also apparent in an oblique, albeit obvious, reference to nineteenth-century pseudo-scientific discourses of race in the poem's focus on gradations of blackness:

> 'You mean – like plain or milk chocolate?' . . .
> 'West African sepia' . . .
> 'Down in the passport.'
> 'Like brunette.'
> 'THAT IS DARK, ISN'T IT?' 'Not altogether.'
> Facially, I am brunette, but madam, you should see
> The rest of me. Palm of my hand, soles of my feet
> Are peroxide blonde. Friction, caused –
> Foolishly madam – by sitting down, has turned
> My bottom raven black – One moment madam! . . .
> 'Wouldn't you rather
> See for yourself'

(Moore 111–12)

The persona subverts the language of racial classification by pretending to take it seriously and applying it not to the differentiation of a whole body from others, as conventional practice would have it, but rather different parts of a single black body, thus turning himself into a multicoloured transgression of the conventional binarism of black and white. Here, we see Soyinka's skill in portraying a serious and sensitive issue in a way that is both funny and critical.

Another early text in which Soyinka displays his immense satirical wit is *The Lion and the Jewel* (1963). In the play, Soyinka conducts a comic dismemberment of a misbegotten cultural project which sets out to reproduce the outer shell rather than the essence of Western modernity, in the course of which it fails signally to take into account, as should be the case, the link between culture and economic as well as technological development. Set against this spirit of uncritical imitation is the old wily Chief Baroka, who teaches the supposedly all-knowing and superior schoolteacher, Lakunle, one or two things about the value of a strategic rather than absolutist cultural location as a vantage point from which to fashion a functionally and workable post-colonial hybrid identity.

The conflict between the two adversaries is carried out over the village beauty, Sidi, who, having been offered, on the one hand, teacher Lakunle's vision of a modernity characterized by, among other things, cutting down trees solely to provide lovers with parks where they can stroll and, on the other, the Baroka's which is predicated on the conservation of the past while selectively adopting elements of the new, chooses the Baroka's way and marries the polygamous village chief rather than the verbose single schoolteacher. That Sidi's choice should be reduced to a consideration of which of the two protagonists is a lesser evil bespeaks the limited nature of the choice offered to her in the play, a choice that suggests that it may not be wrong to regard the play as allegorical.

The depiction of Lakunle as a laughable figure is evident from his general physical presentation, but especially so from the manner of his dress. He is described as

> dressed in an old-style English suit threadbare but not ragged, clean but not ironed, obviously a size or two too small. His tie is done in a very small knot, disappearing beneath a shiny black waistcoat. He wears twenty-three-inch-bottom trousers, and blanco-white tennis shoes.
>
> (SCP 2, 3)

There could be no better way of suggesting that Lakunle is the site of a most odd assembly of cultural time and spatial zones than his wearing an old English suit with tennis shoes. True, cultural hybridity is to be recommended, but Lakunle's stretches the very idea of hybridity to the limit, as if he were mocking the concept itself. The only consolation would be to take the protagonist as representing the subversive mis-identification that characterizes what Homi Bhabha in his *Location of Culture* (1994) describes as 'mimicry', a mode of counter-hegemonic resistance in which colonial discourse's attempt to construct the colonized in terms of its own ideological frame is returned, but in a subversively distorted form. However, given that Lakunle's brand confounds not only the terms of colonial discourse but those of his own local culture, it may be argued that he illustrates the way in which mimicry itself is not singularly, but multiply determined, ambivalently functioning as both a device of resistance and hegemony, for instance. In other words, transferred from the arena of the opposition between the colonized and the coloniser and examined in terms of the local scene, where the choice being made on the extent and content of the appropriation of the Western 'symbolic arbitrary' is part of the project of post-colonial self-determination, mimicry may be less a symptom of the failure of colonial ideological interpellation and more of its successful re-articulation as part of the plurality of the post-colonial discursive formation.[12]

It may also be said that the play dramatizes the degree to which the Western symbolic arbitrary has become the means of reproducing new forms of hierarchial social and political relations within the post-colony. Through the acquisition of the Western alphabet, Lakunle can arrogate to himself powers which he would not have dreamed of having access to within traditional institutions and practices, which points to how literacy and education do not abolish the idea of élitism itself, but merely replace a feudal form of it with a Western one, sometimes producing undemocratic continuities between trad-itional and Western concepts of power. Thus, modernity in this instance merely serves as a site of a new class formation, rather than as the eradication of difference that Lakunle claims it offers.

Furthermore, the view of modernity Lakunle proffers seems to represent some profound confusion over the relationship between modernity and gender equality. In wooing Sidi, he assumes that modernity by its very nature is characterized by a more enlightened gender ideology than tradition. Here are some examples of why Lakunle thinks that is the case:

> Sidi, I seek... an equal partner in my race
> of life...
> When we are wed...
> Together we shall sit at table
> – Not on the floor – and eat,

> Not with fingers, but with knives
> And forks, and breakable plates
> Like civilised beings...
> I want to walk beside you in the street,
> Side by side and arm in arm
> Just like the Lagos couples I have seen
> High-heeled shoes for the lady, red paint
> On the lips.
>
> (SCP 2, 9)

One prays that Sidi does not take Lakunle's advice seriously and apply some red paint to her lips, but even more substantially alarming is that he sees the use of lipstick and what he calls 'breakable plates' as somehow, by virtue of their exoticness, representing a non-patriarchal form of gender ideology. Evidently, Lakunle's idea of equal relations of gender within marriage is based on a superficial reading of the signs of modernity.

At any rate, the liberating modernity Lakunle offers Sidi is constrained by the scientific sexism he has picked up from books. It may thus be argued that in the figure of Lakunle, the conflict between tradition and modernity is reconfigured as a clash of modes of reading: to be precise, as the difference between reading as an uncritical adoption of ideas and reading as a creative translation, or transaction between the reader, including his/her complex cultural background, and the text, and its complex history within a given culture.

Lakunle's merely imitative interpretation of Western texts also affects his understanding of his own culture: he is in many ways the antithesis of Soyinka's idea of an authentic African subject, as he, like other culturally alienated figures in the playwright's work, suffers 'from externally induced fantasies of redemptive transformation in the image of alien masters..., a victim of the doctrine of self-negation' (MLA xii). There is no better evidence of Lakunle's self-negation than the following description of African culture he offers:

> barbaric, out-dated,
> Rejected, denounced, accursed,
> Excommunicated, archaic, degrading,
> Humiliating, unspeakable, redundant,
> Retrogressive, remarkable, unpalatable.
>
> (SCP 2, 8)

It is also noticeable that part of Lakunle's confusion has to do with his assumption that Christianity is the same as civilization and modernity seen, among others, in the following passage:

> Uncivilized and primitive – bush girl!
> I kissed you as all educated men –
> And Christians – kiss their wives.
> It is the way of civilised romance.

(SCP 2 10)

Lakunle's attitude to tradition is also symptomatic of the triumph of a particular form of Christian cultural ideology which regards Christianity as an extension of Western culture. Thus his angle of ideological articulation is the same as that of another of Soyinka's characters, Reverend Erinjobi in *Camwood On the Leaves* (1965), who says more rude things about African culture than any Western missionary would, perhaps. Both characters reproduce a view especially dominant among colonial Christian missionaries and still noticeable in some sections of the post-colonial church in Africa, that all indigenous traditions and practices are evil and that in so far as Christianity disengages people from such practices it represents freedom. As a number of writers have shown, this is not always the case. In Ngugi wa Thiong'o's *The River Between* (1965), for example, it is shown that a fundamentalist Christianity that does not take into account the complex affective relationship between subjects of a given culture and that culture's practices may do more harm than good. That is also the case with Reverend Erinjobi who, in the end, is shot dead by his own son in protest against his overbearing religiosity. Little wonder, then, that Lakunle's Christianized condemnation of tradition brings him very little good either, for such characters, in Soyinka's judgement, are more part of the problem than any radical transformation of post-colonial Africa.

Against this racist and confused view of African culture, we have the Baroka's, which is rendered in the most richly poetic language and which is also firmly located within the local African symbolic arbitrary, evidence of what Soyinka terms 'self-apprehension' (*MLA* xii). As he tells Sidi in the following passage, it is within the traditional structure of thought and belief that Baroka intends to place any new cultural form he encounters, including modernity itself:

16

I do not hate progress, only its nature
Which makes all roofs and faces look the same.
And the wish of one old man is
That...among the bridges and the murderous roads,
Below the humming birds which
Smoke of the face of Shango...we must leave
Virgin plots of leaves, rich decay
And the tang of vapour rising from
Forgotten heaps of compost.

(SCP 2, 47)

In this way, the Baroka comes across as a thoughtful and caring steward of the village and not the reckless destroyer of trees and pretender to the throne of a Lakunle.

However, Soyinka undermines this absolute opposition, by presenting the Baroka as an unscrupulous character who, even within the latitude afforded by tradition, abuses his power. When a British surveyor comes to determine the path of the new railway line, he bribes him away for fear that opening up his village to the wider world may cost him the strong grip he has over his people. Furthermore, when he realizes that Sidi has become more famous than him because of the appearance of her photographs in a city magazine, he connives to share some of her glory by marrying her. Thus, though the Baroka embodies tradition as an antithesis of a ruthlessly negative Western modernity, he is not himself the paradigm of the imagined traditional chiefly grace and uprightness, as he is patently a rogue in a chief's skin. Consequently, despite being the quintessential emancipatory adaptation of African tradition, the Baroka also serves as an example of those characters in Soyinka's work who use tradition merely as one of the means to power. In his case, he uses tradition to humiliate a less experienced male who offers a different and even opposi-tional, albeit confused, form of masculine subjectivity.

Configured as a contest of masculinities, the play is remarkable for its representation of women's identity as merely part of the scene of the conflict between the two men; and there is no suggestion whatsoever that the problem of cultural conflict being staged may be of interest to Sidi and Sadiku (the Baroka's senior wife) as well, in their own right as full subjects of their social formation. Instead, they are wholly presented as

17

extensions of the battle-lines drawn in terms of the differential masculine prowess between Lakunle and Baroka. This is part of the general political blindness of nationalist discourse in Africa, as its primary commitment to the erasure of the Manichean dichotomy of colonial ideology and practice makes it oblivious and even, at times, antagonistic to other forms of political and social difference, such as those of gender and class and, in some cases, even those of ethnicity. In this regard, Soyinka's *The Lion and the Jewel* may very much be a text of its time, when both literature and politics prioritized national independence and the decolonization of the continent over everything else. However, Soyinka has moved on considerably with regard to the question of gender, as indeed he has also in relation to the issue of independence and freedom, as can be seen in his later work such as *Kongi's Harvest* (1967) and *Season of Anomy* (1973).

All said and done, the play shows Soyinka harnessing his powers of satire in order to deflate the self-appointed purveyors of modernity, contending that what sometimes passes off as modernity in Africa, and perhaps elsewhere as well, may be merely half-baked Lakunlean ideas: well-meant, perhaps, but nevertheless utter misreadings of the nature of tradition as well as of the complex needs of the particular formations which such projects are supposed to change for the better. All the same, it is also worth noting that Lakunle's ideas are presented as the excessively zealous views of a country bumpkin who is seduced by the bright lights of the city by virtue of a naivety bred by his rural upbringing. Thus, it may be argued that while the play presents a solid defence of African culture and commendably articulates the need for selective hybridity as a basis for constructing a post-colonial African culture, it also uncritically reproduces the conventional representation of the country and the rural area as backward. As the rural areas of Africa are generally regarded as the custodians of African tradition, such an image does not sit well with the play's cultural nationalism. Even so, what Lakunle stands for is not exclusive to his rural location: it is a madness that ubiquitously takes a variety of forms, as we learn from Soyinka's other works.

One way in which trappings of African modernity become disabling is illustrated by Soyinka's *The Trials of Brother Jero* (1964) and *Jero's Metamorphosis* (1973). Prophet Jeroboam, one of the evangelists roaming a Nigerian beach for converts, is in fact a crook who uses religious language in order to dispossess his converts of cash. It is also worth recalling that evangelical and non-traditional churches were among the groups Soyinka studied as part of his Rockefeller project on African performance traditions and that, according to Robert July, he was extremely impressed by the theatrical qualities of their rituals.[13]

Indeed, Jero is a consummate actor, playing the role of a Christian prophet with impressive credibility. Nevertheless, *The Trials of Brother Jero* is an indictment of a society in which it is no longer possible to differentiate between the sacred and the profane, so much so that ethical contamination or transvaluation can easily pass itself off as progressive cultural hybridity. Jero's adaptation of Christianity to his own local circumstances which, in a different context, would be considered more imaginative than, for example, Lakunle's merely imitative cultural reproduction, here functions as a supreme example of an exploitative false consciousness whereby surplus labour constitutes itself as a parasitic, but nevertheless alternative economy which is itself not free from the fundamental character of the relations of production which have brought it into being. The beach has thus become the simulation of the politics and corruption of the higher orders of society.

The emptiness of Jero's religious rhetoric resembles that of nationalist ideology whose promises were proving patently false or simply untenable by the time Soyinka was writing the play, as corruption aided by ethnicity began to undermine the moral fibre of the post-colonial nation. In this context, Soyinka sought to foreground the political subtext of *The Trials of Brother Jero* more overtly by having Jero deliberately modelling himself on the new military leadership which had seized power from a civilian government in 1965, and we are told in *Jero's Metamorphosis* that 'the large uniformed figure at a battery of microphones', in a picture on the wall in Jero's office, 'indicates that Jero's diocese is no longer governed by his old friends the civilian politicians' (*SCP* 2, 42). In keeping with the changed times, Jero describes himself as an Office General, arguing that he may as well be one since it is the fashion of the day.

Jero has also adopted the civil service parlance, and is not a pushover when it comes to engaging in civil-service-speak when trying to get the government officials to lease the beach to him rather than the Salvation Army, which the government regards as likely to make it more respectable than the prophets would. Of equal significance is the way he mixes together the language of military and religious power, focusing on their external form rather than content. However, in a world where generals are no longer in charge of armies, but are waging war against the national treasury, Jero's chameleon-like identity is less of an aberration than the defining norm.

Jero finds the ideal combination of religious and military identity in the practices of the Salvation Army; thus, once he has successfully blackmailed the government official into signing away the beach to him, he forms a similar type of band composed of the criminal brotherhood of the beach prophets, over whom he now has the absolute control of a dictator. He seems to have learnt a lot from those in power. The ease with which he manages to make his organization publicly respectable shows that a corrupt political set-up may fool some people all the time, but that it will not fool a Jero even once, as he will not only use such power parasitically, but also embarrass it by nonchalantly dramatizing what a good student he has been. Indeed, this is the point he makes when he and his gang of fellow-robbers celebrate the formation of their new upmarket outfit for extorting money from beach users:

> We shall manifest our united spiritual essence in the very form and shape of the rulers of the land. Nothing, you will agree could be more respectable than that. Sister Rebecca, bring out the banner!

REBECCA. Is this the moment, Brother Jero?

JERO. The moment is now, Sister. Witness the birth of the first Church of the Apostolic Salvation Army of the Lord!... Forward into the battle, Brothers.

ISAAC. Against what?...

JERO. Precisely. Against what? We don't know any more than our secular models. They await a miracle, we will provide it.

(*SCP* 2, 205)

Jero is not only the mirror image of the national leadership, but he presents himself as the solution they have been waiting for, a sort of extreme carnivalesque satirization of politics, religion, law and morality.

In the plays, it is not so much Jero who is the butt of the satire, but rather the leadership of his country, of which he is an unusual but, all the same, close imitation. The leaders are so corrupt that a man like Jero who flaunts his vices without a scintilla of embarrassment comes across as more sincere than those who, like the government officials we see in the play, revel in hypocrisy. With the Jero plays, Soyinka had begun to evolve a satirical style which explored the potential for grotesque extremity of corrupt post-colonial power. As is noticeable from *A Play of Giants* (1984), this type of satire also operates with a shocking normalization of the abnormally extreme. In this particular instance, Soyinka uses the technique to poke fun at dictatorship which is presented as if it were not unusual, but rather the most ordinary of situations; and by being presented in this manner, its oddity is made more poignant than would otherwise be the case.

The play is about a private conference of four notorious African dictators who are in New York for a United Nations meeting. As Soyinka admits in the preface, the four dictators are based on former African leaders: Macias Nguema of Equatorial Guinea, Emperor Jean-Baptiste Bokassa of the Central African Republic, Mobuto Sese Seko of Zaire, and Idi Amin of Uganda. The meeting is being held at the private quarters of the Embassy of the worst of the four, Kamini, modelled on Idi Amin. As the meeting progresses, the dictator becomes more and more paranoid, and, when he gets news that he has been toppled in a *coup d'état*, he takes his fellow dictators and high-ranking American and Soviet Union officials as well as the Secretary-General of the United Nations hostage. On the basis of the manner of his own ascendancy to power, he argues that it is certain that one of the superpowers has sponsored the coup and that if the two superpowers do not undo it, he will fire the guns he has already trained at the United Nations Building just opposite. When the Embassy is invaded by exiles from his country he carries out his threat.

The play sets African political power in the global context of Cold War politics in which most regimes were pawns, and often willing ones, in an agenda far removed from the concerns of their own people and one in which an obviously amoral dictator such as Idi Amin was not short of friends, having been supported by

21

Britain, America, and the Soviet Union, as well as the Organization of African Unity, at different stages of his career. By having such a dictator destroy the United Nations building, Soyinka is suggesting that such leaders have the capacity of causing mischief not only in their own backyard, but also internationally. In the context of the 1992 Gulf War, the play can be read as a very perceptive study of Third World dictatorships and their complex relations with Western governments.

It is not only Western governments that are co-opted in the production and maintenance of African dictatorships, but also certain sections of the Western intellectual class represented by Gudrum, a Scandinavian artist and Kamini's biographer, who is approvingly described by Kamini as follows:

> Gudrum, a very good friend of African leaders. She writing book about me many photographs. She calling it, *The Black Giant at Play*. It show Kamini very very jovial family man. Big uncle to everybody in country.

> *(PG 2)*

Gudrum symbolizes the non-institutional international support given to African dictators, and, in her case, the admiration for Kamini is based on a certain primitivist valorization of his self-representation as the equivalent of a modern-day 'noble savage', amoral and unconstrained by any social norms of behaviour. That Kamini is ungovernably beyond rules of normal etiquette is amply evident in a scene where he is defecating in full view of one of his guests and, in fact, continues conversing while so engaged. As it happens, the guest is the sculptor sent by Madame Tussaud's in London to make a statue of the dictator for its African section. However, Kamini hijacks the idea and orders him to do a sculpture of him in the company of his fellow dictators, and further insists that it should be done within two days or so for it to be exhibited, not in Madame Tussaud's as arranged but in the United Nations building itself. The sculptor's joke about Kamini's statue being more suitable for the chamber of horrors than anything else, confided in Gudrum and divulged to the dictator, earns him a beating, proving that in Kamini's residence even foreigners are subjected to his local brand of justice.

The dictator's sadistic nature is clearly demonstrated when

Gudrum tells him about some of the exiles living in her country who oppose him. He does not mince words as to what he is going to do with them: 'All subversives bad people. Mostly imperialist agents. Better you kill them first' (PG 3). He is also shown to treat the Governor of his Central Bank with exceptional cruelty when the latter explains that the World Bank cannot give Bugara a loan because Kamini has just been printing money without due regard to the relevant international regulations. In Kamini's view, so long as he has paper and a printing machine, he does not see why he should be short of money, and anyone complicating this simple truth, as the governor does, is subversive. Kamini has his bodyguards take him to the toilet and push his head under the toilet bowl. This form of extreme cruelty is reminiscent of Amin's exceptional viciousness and also of his alleged cannibalism, tales of which were the staple of the international media and which he himself did very little to discourage as they sowed fear among those opposed to him.

It is also significant that Soyinka includes among supporters of Kamini the African-American Professor Batey, for whom Kamini is a paradigm of African authenticity. This is an allusion propagated by the former president of Zaire, Mobuto Sese Seko, to a form of Negritude called *authenticité* to which was no more than an attempt to entrench and legitimize his power through the language of tradition, thereby presenting any criticism of his regime from the perspective of modern principles of democracy as a sign of cultural alienation. Such manipulation of tradition has also been used by other dictators, such as the former president of Malawi, Hastings Banda. However, unproblematically transferred to particular diasporic sites of anti-racism, such assertions of African authenticity by dictators can seem radical and lead to the unwitting validation of intra-racial oppressive relations. So, like Gudrum, Professor Batey too is writing a book about Kamini entitled *The Black Giant at Work*, presenting him as a symbol of black power.

Furthermore, the play also reveals that there is no limit to the violence of dictatorship, as the mini-summit of dictators regresses into a nursery-school-type competition over who is the meanest of them all. Soyinka presents the dictators as laughably infantile while also exposing their fetishization of power and status as a pathological desire to be in control, itself driven by their knowledge of the ubiquity of the so-called subversives who haunt them even as they bask in the safety of each other's company and the institutional prestige of the United Nations. They all have groups attempting to topple them, and the fear of being ousted from power drives them to an inordinate obsession with holding onto it.

Indeed, it may be argued that it is in an attempt to outdo the other dictators that the host dictator decides to hold his colleagues hostage, showing them that he is rather more of a dictator than they are. Even so, the fact that personal power rather than a general social good becomes the privileged site of competition among this august assembly indicates the extent to which the crisis of governance in the African post-colony may significantly have to do with the dissolution of the boundary between the private and the public spheres. A major consequence of this state of affairs is that the sudden departure from power of an individual, such as Said Barre of Somalia or Mobuto Sese Seko of Zaire, inexorably leads to the collapse of public institutions; inevitable because, under a dictatorship, the public space is merely the extension of individualized power.

In the play Soyinka demonstrates that there is more at stake in a dictatorship than the violation of human rights, as the dictator contracts the life-span of public institutions to that of his regime and thus inscribes himself not only on the present, but also on the future of the nation, forcing it to start all over again or disintegrate further after his departure. In essence, it is the idea of dictatorship as the nonchalant personalization of public time and space by an individual that is dramatized in Soyinka's satire. His conviction that the problem deserves more study is evident in the theme's reappearance in his long satirical play, *Opera Wonyosi* (1977).

Opera Wonyosi is an imaginative adaptation of John Gay's eighteenth-century classic, *The Beggar's Opera*, and Bertolt Brecht's *Threepenny Opera*. As the playwright puts it in the preface, 'Opera Wonyosi is an exposition of levels of power in practice – by a satirist pen...as a prerequisite of the land's transformation' (*SSP* 300). The play's revelatory concern is with the foregrounding of the erasure of difference between the criminal and the politician, showing how the men of power, as one character puts it, criminal or otherwise, speak a common language. As far as Soyinka is concerned, the street gangsters are simply reproducing on the lower levels what is being practised in high places; indeed, just as in *Jero's Metamorphosis*, it is the criminals' awareness that this is so that gives them even more influence on the leadership and additionally makes them more daring in their exploits, for they reckon that the agencies of law enforcement are more likely to enforce illegality for a good fee than they are to enforce the law itself. In this way breaking the law as a practice is normalized by being accorded the conventional status of formality reserved for law-enforcement.

The inseparability of the criminal and the politician is also a subject of comic confusion for the DEE JAY (the master of ceremonies), who is compelled to rehearse the difficulty of giving the opera a name that best describes its principal protagonist:

> I'm hosting this show. One time called it *Way-Out Opera*, – for short, *Opera Wayo*. Call it the *Beggar's Opera* if you insist – that is what the whole nation is doing – begging for a slice of the action.... And don't think it is the kind of begging you're used to. Here the beggars say, 'Give me a slice of action, or... give me a slice of your throat'... I've yet to decide whether such a way-out opera should be named after the beggars, the army, the bandits, the police, the cash-madams, the students, the trades-unionists, the Alhajis and Alhajas, the Aladura, the academicals, the Holy Radicals...
>
> (SSP 303)

Nevertheless, though the whole nation is involved in this unholy begging, it is the similarity between the gangster and the political beggars that is most thoroughly examined in the play, especially their extravagant lifestyles and manipulation of power.

In the play, the president of the country has decided to turn himself into a monarch, and since he has got rid of all the opposition and the country is virtually a police state, there is no longer anyone who can oppose his growing appetite for new forms of aggrandizement and display of power. His coronation is a good opportunity for him to show off his taste in royal regalia and food. It is, however, ironic that the audience is only privy to the monarch's delicate choice of food through the feast being held by Captain Macheath, Mackie for short, and his royal entourage of the most notorious villains in the land. The emperor would perhaps regret the loss of his imported food, but he would certainly not be disappointed by the cultured table manners of the gentlemen of violence gathered for Mackie's wedding. Their flair for sophistication is explicit in their attempt to impress Polly with the royal origin of her wedding utensils and food:

BABA.   Splendid plates. From the Hotel Intercontinental. Same firm as makes the Emperor's cutlery.

DARE.   To tell you the truth, ma'am. Everything is the same as the Emperor will have on his coronation. The salmon is from Lafayette, by special appointment Fishmongers to His Imperial Majesty. Specially flown from France last night. No problem slipping in among the crates at the airport. Came through the VIP lounge – a Right Royal Salmon I tell you.

(SSP 322)

It is not easy to condemn Captain Mackie's and his assistants' theft of the food destined for the emperor's unjustifiably expensive and wasteful coronation, as their behaviour is really not different from the emperor's raiding of the nation's coffers in order to pay for his infantile wish to be an emperor. Now, if corruption in a society makes it difficult to separate the criminals from the lawmakers, it is little wonder that the master of ceremonies has trouble deciding who precisely to name his show after.

Another link between the criminals, the political leadership, and the civil service is revealed when war breaks out between Chief Anikura, Polly's father and a gangster, and Captain Mackie, over the latter's marriage to Polly without her father's consent. Anikura fears that his daughter's marriage to a rival gangster will render him vulnerable to exploitation and manipulation. In order to stop the marriage he blackmails Mackie's police protector into arresting him for numerous murders he has committed in the past, but out of which he has successfully managed to bribe his way. He is to be publicly executed as part of the emperor's coronation. It is thus clear that the state apparatuses are not only at the mercy of the gangsters, but that the state itself is a gangster. In this sense, one is no longer dealing with a case such as Jero's, whereby a criminal takes advantage of state corruption, but rather with a situation in which gangsterism is both state ideology and practice.

The public's enthusiasm for the Captain's public execution is further indication of the erosion of respect for human life in the society depicted in *Opera Wonyosi*, and also of the widespread affective involvement of the population at large in the public rituals of state brutality. Luckily for Mackie, as he is awaiting his execution before a crowd baying for blood, a messenger delivers the emperor's pardon offered to celebrate his coronation. Chief Anikura warns the masses that they should not regard the Captain's pardon as normal and hope that they will be similarly treated – he is a man of power, and that makes a huge difference in this self-styled empire.

However, with absolute power comes a fetishization of violence itself. In one instance we see the emperor arbitrarily selecting his victim with his eyes closed, suggesting that he no longer needs an excuse or a reason to subject anyone to violence. In another incident, he threatens a hapless aide with being sent as a present to his friend Idi Amin after the aide mistakenly, and in eagerness to please, addresses him as 'emperor' before the official coronation. Soyinka recalls a painful event when a renowned Ugandan writer, who had supported Idi Amin initially, told him on his way into exile that at first one had known what to avoid, but later it was difficult to know what could get one into trouble.[14] In this respect the play continues Soyinka's representation of the unpredictable potential for violence of dictatorial power dramatized in *A Play of Giants*. However, it is also noticeable that in this instance he goes a bit further, edging closer to the bitter condemnation of human folly and vice more characteristic of his juvenalian moments than his usual cheerful style, making *Opera Wonyosi* more akin to his tragicomedies than such examples of light satire as *The Lion and the Jewel* with which we began the chapter.

Clearly, Soyinka has the undoubted ability to offer serious social and political commentary through a variety of satirical styles and, as such, critics who claim that he is difficult to read perhaps would do better to start with his comedies and satires. Nor would one agree with Ngugi's observation that Soyinka leaves the masses as pitiful comedians on the road; in fact, he shows them imaginatively reading and adapting to the different languages of power, showing that, though they may be marginal, they are not always simply victims.[15] Soyinka's principal concern in the satires is thus to show how, once corruption is fully entrenched in a particular social formation, it is not easily understood in terms of familiar social and political categories, for they are often in such circumstances themselves infused with the hegemonic values of corruption. Also, satire provides the writer with the means of problematizing the relationship between tradition and modernity in a way that neither wholly romanticizes the former nor demonizes the latter. Yet, as will be shown in Chapter 3, his satire can be bitter and anguished at times.

3

Tragic Comedies and Comic Tragedies

A number of Soyinka's texts cannot easily be categorized as either comedy or tragedy. These transgeneric, or in-between, texts exhibit a productive immanent tension between the two modes of representation, emphasizing the complexity not only of the post-colonial experience itself, but also of the writer's own attitude to it. This combination of the comic and the tragic is, as Mark Kinkead-Weekes and Femi Abodunrin point out, an important structural device in Soyinka's works. Kinkead-Weekes illuminatingly remarks that Soyinka has the knack, especially in his plays, of 'using a two-part structure to transform our view of what we have been watching: a first part satiric, comic and done in human terms; a second part tragic, mythic, and aware of forces and perspectives beyond human terms' (Gibbs 2, 229).[1] Useful as Kinkead-Weekes' observations are, they are not true of most of Soyinka's plays, particularly the ones examined in the previous chapter or those, such as *The Strong Breed*, which will be considered in the next. Moreover, it is the dual presence of identifiable conventional genres as well as mixed ones in Soyinka's creative corpus that testifies not only to his exceptional ability to recreate the literary tradition, but also to his superb mastery of it, so much so that his departures from the norm are recognizably those of someone who has learnt his trade well, rather than one who is propelled by ignorance of literary history or by its wilful disregard.

A text that marks a significant shift in Soyinka's approach to the question of generic identity is *Kongi's Harvest*, written in the mid-sixties and first directed by the author in 1966. It is conceivable that the 1965 military takeover of government in

Nigeria, together with Soyinka's growing realization that the nationalist leadership had been engaged in elaborately eccentric forms of despotism and corruption, prompted him to seek a new representational mode. This new language is committed to a full and total revelation of the foundations as well as the surface manifestations of tyranny and greed, for, as Soyinka himself puts it, 'when power is placed in the service of vicious reaction, a language must be called into being which does its best to appropriate such obscenity of power and fling its excesses back in its face,' making 'language . . . a part of resistance therapy' (*SCP* 2, xiv). Significantly, this is also the view Soyinka takes in his preface to *Opera Wonyosi*, a play that is wholly satirical, as nothing drastic happens to any of the principal characters in the end, but one which evidently has a bitter edge to it. Nevertheless, the bitterness and gloom of *Opera Wonyosi* are surpassed in *Kongi's Harvest*.

Nowhere is this pessimism more explicit than in the invincibility of the dictator of the Republic of Isma. Kongi is a post-colonial leader who has just ascended to power having prosecuted a successful war of decolonization. It has been widely speculated that Soyinka's dictator is based on Kwame Nkrumah and Hastings Banda, respectively the first post-colonial leaders of Ghana and Malawi.[2] Both had a penchant for style, and it is the obsession with self-presentation that afflicts Kongi, with most of the play taken up with his preparation for the public meeting where, forcibly, but with the seeming consent of Oba Danlola, he will take over the emblems and symbols of traditional power, thus removing the only source of institutionalized opposition.

The main target of the satire in the first part of the play is Kongi's preoccupation with fashioning himself into an imagined omnipotent leader; and, as we see the lengths to which he will go in order to effect such a transformation, we become aware of the pathological nature of his obsession, and laughter gives way to the realization that such madness is not only funny but destructive. When the play opens, Kongi and members of his Reformed Awerri Fraternity, his replacement for the Oba's Awerri Council, are in a mountain retreat preparing themselves for his public investiture as the new national leader. However, it is noteworthy that the most important item on the agenda is that of finding a suitable image for the regime, including the cabinet's, as we learn from one of the ministers:

FOURTH AWERRI.   We need an image. Tomorrow being our first appearance in public, it is essential that we find an image...Magi is more dignified. We hold, after all, the position of the wise ones. From the recognition of us as the Magi, it is one step to his inevitable apotheosis.

(SCP 2, 70)

By the time the Fourth Awerri proposes that their 'pronouncements should be dominated by a positive scientificism' (SCP 2, 71), it becomes even more evident that Soyinka is here caricaturing Kwame Nkrumah's political theory, which he termed 'consciencism'. What is also obviously contradictory is that 'positive scientificism' is adopted for reasons which are so self-evidently illogical:

SIXTH.   What image is positive scientificism?
THIRD.   Whatever it is, it is not long-winded proverbs and senile pronouncements. In fact, as we could say, a step has already been taken in that direction. If you have read our Leader's last publication...
FIFTH.   Ah yes. Nor proverbs nor verse, only ideograms in algebraic quantums. If the square of XjQY (2bc) equals QA into the square root of X, then the progressive forces will prevail over the reactionary in the span of .32 of a single generation.

(SCP 2, 72)

It is clear that an image is chosen that appears to fit Kongi's muddled conception of the relationship between politics and science. The Reformed Awerri's obsession with Gradgrindian exactitude suggests that this might equally be an example of the Dickensian influence on Soyinka that James Gibbs mentions in his study of the writer.[3] As in Dickens's Hard Times, so here the cobbling together of incongruous ideas in the name of science does lead to a tragic end. In addition, Kongi's easy acceptance of anything that is opposed to tradition as a fitting philosophy for the new regime may also be regarded as a sign of the uncritical privileging of modernity over tradition that is the hallmark of Lakunle's project. Besides, it is a matter of the past haunting the present, as Kongi and his Reformed Awerri feel deeply insecure about how they measure up to the old order of Oba Danlola and his Awerri council.

Equally noticeable is that the Reformed Awerri are themselves at the mercy of the dictator. For instance, the choice of the image for the regime is based more on sycophantic considerations than any others, and the desire to please Kongi arises out of constantly living in fear of his unpredictably irrational punitiveness. They have good cause to be afraid of him, as someone who has forced them to fast for the sake of coming up with an image of the regime: 'fasting under duress', as one of the most hungry Awerri puts it, could easily destroy them physically. In this regard they are not different from Oba Danlola, whom Kongi has imprisoned for refusing to hand over to him the role of the spirit of the Yam Harvest festival, which involves ritualistically blessing the largest yam in the land. To some extent the Oba is freer because he knows that his imprisonment is for a sound principle; but the starving Reformed Awerri have to invent a principle to justify not only the regime's existence, but also their own committee's; nevertheless, even when they do so, the vacuity of it all cannot escape them.

In fact Kongi's arrogance is such that he no longer even allows them the fiction of autonomy or the mask of being advisers – increasingly, he simply tells them what to do. After their long sleepless deliberations on the image of the regime, they are told by the secretary that 'the Leader's image for the next Five-Year Development Plan will be that of a benevolent father of the nation... The Keyword is Harmony' (SCP 2, 76). Contrary to what they think, it is not as wise men or magi that Kongi sees them, but rather as automata he can bend at will, and also as punch-bags on which he can practise his autocratic rule and make necessary improvements on it, if need be. For Daodu, the heir to Danlola's throne, and Segi, Kongi's former mistress and now Daodu's girlfriend, Kongi's growing dictatorship must be stopped at once.

As satire gives way to a sombre acknowledgement of the wanton destructiveness of Kongi's power and as, furthermore, his adversaries' plans to oust him become more and more elaborate, the reader or audience becomes aware that the initial comic dismemberment of Kongi was but a prelude to the violent eruption of what the dictator had hitherto repressed. In the end, the Festival is marred by an assassination attempt on Kongi by

Segi's father, who is himself killed by Kongi's guards. Then Segi offers Kongi a copper salver containing her father's severed head instead of the expected big yam. Kongi is bewildered and outraged, but not cowed.

His indestructibility is proven by the fact that he manages to bring everything under control and, in a typical dictator's style, a number of former trusted officials, including his mouthpiece, the organizing secretary, are on the run for fear that his paranoid disposition might point the finger of blame at them and have them executed. Also heading for exile are Segi and Daodu, who realize that they tried, but have failed miserably to unseat Kongi and that he will kill them if they remain in Isma. Thus the point is made that corrupt leadership may start off as a minor laughable eccentricity, but can hatch into a monstrous cannibalism, which is alluded to in the presentation of the severed head to Kongi. However, once such heights of violence, symbolic or otherwise, have been reached, it becomes difficult to determine the most humane way of getting rid of the dictator, and Soyinka does not offer any clear solution to the problem. Nevertheless, the fact that a variety of Kongi's former enemies go together into exile across the border suggests the possibility of a new alliance of counter-Kongi forces which may return to haunt the dictator and even get rid of him ultimately.

It is in Soyinka's novel *The Interpreters* (1965), published a year before *Kongi's Harvest* was first performed, that we are offered a study of how a corrupt post-colonial culture can sap the zeal and energy of some of its best potential leaders. Combining satire and tragedy, the novel focuses on a group of young Nigerian intellectuals who have just returned from overseas study, full of hope and enthusiasm for the development of their country. However, it soon dawns on them that the society to which they have returned is rotten to the core and that any hope of standing above it all is not only unrealistic, but quite dangerous.

Sekoni, the visionary engineer, is assigned low-grade clerical work instead of the tasks he is employed for, and when, in a fit of rebelliousness, he challenges his board of directors to give him an appropriate job, he is sent to build a power station in a remote village, something that he is very excited about but which proves to be his undoing. Once he has completed the station his superiors hire an expatriate consultant at great expense whose brief is simply to use the prestige of being from abroad to legitimize the board's condemnation of the plant as hazardous. It is clear that they are doing it to spite Sekoni for daring to be different from the other employees; but, most important of all to them, a condemned power station is more profitable than a working one, as they are able to claim a lot of money on it. And when Sekoni tries to resurrect his project, he is arrested and sent to a mental hospital.

There are many instances of such corruption in the novel, but the challenge for the been-toos, who are expected to do something about it, is exactly how to relate to this extreme situation of moral decadence.[4] The small coterie of intellectual friends, Sekoni, Segoe, Egbo, Dehinwa, Bendele, and Kola, withdraws from the world in a variety of ways. Principally, they find refuge in a language of distanciation, dominated by wit, irony, satire, and insincere hyperbole. Yet, even as language shields them from the reality of their existence, it also constantly betrays their repressed anxiety. For instance, when Egbo, the heir to the throne of Osa, who had been sent overseas to study by his community in the hope that when he returned they would have an educated leader, fails to decide between his paper-pushing job in the foreign office and the throne, he is able to treat his predicament with an accomplished flippancy. The weighty choice facing him is lost in petty semantic quibbling over the relationship between 'apostate' and 'apostasy', and finally, when one of his friends asks whether he has made up his mind which way they are going with their boat, he replies simply, 'With the tide', which sums up the life of all the interpreters in the novel. They will flow with the general tide until it spews them out.

Nevertheless, the interpreters' identification with the system is not always uncritical. In Egbo's case, the rejection of a traditional title is based on the fact that he will most obviously be a bandit chief, since from time immemorial the chiefdom has been used for smuggling, and the royal family has always been part of this trade, as the size of chiefdom militates against putting up any form of resistance against the myriad traffickers who use it. Soyinka thus complicates the relationship between tradition and modernity, for the traditional world Egbo is invited to join is not dissimilar in its corruption from the urban places. Nor is there the fiction here of some idyllic moment in the past when the kingdom was a paradigm of the sort of moral virtue one associates with rural or traditional communities. Yet, in the complex games of rationalization played by the interpreters, even Egbo himself casts doubt on the sincerity of his excuse, but he lacks the courage to break out of the rhetorical cocoon he and his fellow interpreters have woven around themselves. This suggests that the interpreters' flaw is that they have collectively deprived themselves of the will to act by fashioning existential apathy into a political ideology, and, in their rejection of agency and the acceptance of voluntarism they bear a strong resemblance to protagonists of existentialist classics such as Albert Camus' *The Outsider* and Samuel Beckett's *Waiting For Godot*.

Like Camus' hero, Meursault, one of the ways in which the interpreters locate themselves outside dominant social values is by being spectacularly unconventional. In this regard Segoe's deflation of upper-class pomposity is aptly illustrative. When Bendele, the lecturer, invites the journalist to the Vice-Chancellor's house, Segoe reacts badly to his hosts' imitation of upper-class British social rituals and mannerisms. The house is described as a 'petrified forest' for its plastic plants and fruit. In protest and under the influence of drink, Segoe plucks the plastic apples and throws them through the window. His anger is directed not only at the tuxedoed Professor Oguazor, but also at the condescending hangers-on surrounding him, such as his English son-in-law, Pinkshore. Segoe's distaste for Africans trying to be more English than the English is buttressed by the efforts of an ally from the very social group he is denouncing. Monica, the English wife of the most obvious social climber and keen observer of the local version of English etiquette, Professor Faseyi, resists Mrs Oguazor's attempts to get her to behave in a ladylike fashion:

> 'My dear, you are being very awkward. All the ladies retire upstairs at this point...'
> 'But I don't want to go upstairs.'
> 'These details of common etiquette cannot be really strange to you. And if they are, simply watch the others and follow their example.... Perhaps, you would like to adjust your make-up.'
> 'But I don't use make-up...'

'You will come with me at once ... or don't ever expect to be invited to my house again.'

(*I.* 145–6)

It is indeed one of the many instances of intense irony in the novel to see an African woman trying to return the supposedly wayward Monica to her upper-class English heritage. Her husband, whose ambition is to use his university post as a stepping-stone to a more lucrative job with a multinational company or a similar organization, apologizes to the Vice-Chancellor for his wife's uncultured behaviour. However, Monica has already fallen in love with a similarly anti-establishment interpreter – Kola, the artist.

Overall, the episode shows that behind the veneer of politeness and cultivation there lurks violence: the Oguazors and Pinkshores are not immune to fighting back with all the means at their disposal when their cultural assumptions are questioned. In the end it is difficult to tell whether, apart from gloves and tuxedos, this class is really as different from the rest of the country as it seeks to present itself. Moreover, one is never certain why the interpreters frequent such parties. Bendele's excuse that 'don't you enjoy just watching people sometimes, especially when you know they can't stand the sight of you?' (*I.* 143) rings hollow. It all suggests that the interpreters are not as different from what they regard as corrupt society as they imagine themselves to be, thus implying that they suffer from the same delusion of absolute difference as the Oguazors' social group. They might be described as occupying a 'false margin', since they are fascinated by and derive enormous pleasure from mixing with the rich and famous, and such occasions afford them a refreshing change from the humdrum routine of their usual leaking haunt. It may also be said that being on the margin of this social world gives them a much-needed sense of moral superiority, a space where they can experience an imaginary political agency as they are allowed to see themselves as revolutionaries. Clearly, it does not take a lot to come across as radical in the company of Oguazor and Pinkshore. It is a measure of the utter feebleness of the interpreters' revolutionary gestures that Segoe's way of getting at the class enemy is by hitting Pinkshore with a plastic fruit. If the interpreters are the redeemers that society had been waiting for, it is not clear in what direction they would lead it and, in the end, the tragedy of their condition is that they are not the hope for the future, but, if anything, an example of its obvious bleakness.

The interpreters have achieved the magnitude of vacuity that Kola ascribes to Noah who has no identity of his own but mediates other people's supremely. This is most evident in their attempts to ground their cynicism in metaphysical interpretative schemes. Segoe has written what he terms a 'Book of Enlightenment' which contains his philosophy of 'voidancy'. It is evidently an expression of the avoidance of engagement with the immediate in which the interpreters indulge, but it is also, especially, in its Lakunlean verbosity, an indication of how excessive reification of a particular concrete situation can mask the abdication of political agency. Surely, presenting the following to a half-literate messenger such as Matthew is not the pedagogy of the oppressed, but is rather oppressing them by means of a delusive pedagogy:

> And silence is to the Voidante as the fumes of opium are to the mystics of the Orient. The silence of the lavatory in an English suburban house when the household and the neighbours have departed to their daily toil, and the guest voidates alone.... And the vows of silence. Above all else, the vows of silence must be kept. Against love, against need and the willingness to give.
>
> (I. 96–7)

Thus, once again, Soyinka pokes fun at the tendency towards homespun philosophies in the post-colony and the mingling of ideas from different traditions without any care for their individual histories and contexts. This is similar to Kongi's 'positive scientifism'. Apart from Segoe's, we have Sekoni's idea of the infinite dome of harmony, which we never get to hear fully because his severe stutter makes it impossible for him to explain it at length, and so it is issued in painful short bursts and one's understanding of it never improves with further explanation. Like Segoe's 'voidancy', here chaff and wheat are so intermingled that the labour of separation would be Herculean. The issue here is not the complexity of ideas, but rather it is the practice of turning abstract reasoning into an undifferentiated end in itself.

In addition to the interpreters, there are others who attempt to construct meaningful identities. Like the albinos, Lazarus and the girl who poses for Kola's painting of the Yoruba pantheon, Joe Golder is one of the many characters in the novel who falls between stools, and through them Soyinka presents the in-between space as not itself homogenous, but rather as variously constituted and not always disadvantageously. This is certainly the case with Lazarus, who uses his being an albino to enhance his prophetic credentials, as well as with Joe Golder, who can endlessly position himself advantageously. For example, within the discourse of national identity he can, as an American, criticize the Africans, the British, and the French, but he can also easily shift into that of race and regard himself as one with the Africans in relation to white America. However, Golder's awareness of the fact that his blackness is not quite self-evident and that, for most Africans he meets, he is white, turns him into a fundamentalist exponent of the doctrine of 'black is beautiful'. What is revealed here is the anxiety of in-betweenness, especially when it is experienced less as a positive identity than as an absence of the definiteness of what are perceived as authentic identities.

His sexuality adds further complexity to his identity. His valorization of the black body is partial, as it focuses solely on the male body; and, in a culture where homosexuality is either discouraged or openly condemned, he is an outsider, just like the interpreters. Most of the interpreters accept his sexuality, except when his attempt to entice a young man ends in the youth's death. The incident brings to the surface some of the profound ideological differences among the interpreters. Egbo, for instance, refuses to share the same car with Golder, and furthermore takes exception to Bendele's and Kola's attempts to protect him from the law by falsifying evidence. Nevertheless, Golder's desire to integrate himself in the community fails as he finds himself, like the interpreters, outside society. Even then, there are signs towards the end of the novel that the interpreters' self-imposed exile, unlike Golder's forced exclusion, is coming to an end.

The shallowness of the interpreters' existence is brought home when Sekoni dies in a car accident, and their encounter with Prophet Lazarus, a Jero-like figure, provides the first moment for questioning the adequacy of their approach to life. Bendele gives up being cynical, and, when asked whether or not he believes in Lazarus's claim to having resurrected from the dead, he tells his colleagues they are not entitled to subject his story to ridicule, for if it works for him they should not tamper with it. The interpreters are changing not only in relation to their wholesale cynical disregard of all views incompatible with theirs, but also in their attitude to power. Egbo admits, 'My rejection of power was thoughtless ... If you seek to transform, you must not be afraid of power. Take Lazarus' (*I.* 182). This process of transformation leads to what is described as a night of 'severance', with the individual interpreters for the first time standing up for what they believe and finding that when they do so with passion their friendship is heavily tested.

On the whole, *The Interpreters* portrays the violence of language, particularly when it is used as a mode of self-defence against one's failure to act. It also illustrates how self-deflation and irony, which afford the principal characters much pleasure, can serve as symptoms of a deeply repressed anguish rather than as signs of sophisticated wit. Indeed, the tragic essence of the play is that the characters delude themselves that the invisibility of the hopelessness which they hide under glibness and a cheerful cynicism is indicative of its absence, and thus do not realize until much too late that it always returns, in a Freudian manner, with a vengeance. It may additionally be argued that the novel is also an exhortation to worry less about style and more about the substance of ideology, and it is in the recognition and implementation of this truth that the rebirth of a decaying post-colonial society can begin in earnest. On a more general level, *The Interpreters* questions the validity of those aspects of existentialist philosophy that emphasize the acceptance of the human condition, with all its suffering, without providing the means of its transcendence.

Indeed, the acceptance of the human condition without an accompanying desire for its transformation is shown to lead to misanthropy and cannibalism in Soyinka's *Madmen and Specialists*, a play which, like *The Interpreters*, is concerned with how language conceals the real content of particular ideological practices and their corresponding forms of subjectivity. As in other texts discussed in this chapter, the play exhibits Soyinka's trained eye for the comic potential of even the most tragic situation, but the laughter it induces is not of the lightness evoked by *The Lion and The Jewel* or *The Trials of Brother Jero*, for example, but the heavier kind associated with Soyinka's favourite character, Shakespeare's King Lear, when in his royal madness he outperforms his own fool. Lear commands our pity, and is thus a tragic hero, but Dr Bero, the specialist, evokes horror, for he lacks the redeeming grace of human frailty of a Lear, suffering as he does from an acute form of hubris which, like that of Marlowe's Dr Faustus, insatiably drives him to seek the acquisition of all available knowledge for the sake of the power it promises rather than for its social value. If the analogy between the play and *King Lear* be carried a little further, it could be said that it is in Bero's father, Old Man, that we see the humanizing and liberatory function of madness.

During a civil war, reminiscent of the 1966–70 Nigerian civil war, Dr Bero, an ambitious young medical doctor, joins the army as a member of the medical corps; but then, in his relentless pursuit of power, he enlists for the army intelligence services, in the course of which he turns his medical knowledge into the state's instrument of torture and death. Bero keeps his sister and his father in the dark about his real job, mostly dwelling on the horrors of war in his letters home. Hearing of the atrocities being committed at the war front, Old Man, the father, decides that if human beings are going to kill one another in such large numbers, they might as well be encouraged to practise cannibalism so that the produce of their murderous labour is not wasted. He joins the army with the immediate aim of helping the wounded, but also with the long-term objective of demonstrating that cannibalism is the only logical and civilized outcome of purposeless warfare. Indeed, the opportunity for Old Man to inculcate his philosophy of 'As' arises when he is put in charge of the rehabilitation of the wounded, whom he puts beyond all fear: the fear of cannibalism, the fear of death and, subversively, the fear of state violence. It is this secret that Bero and the state want desperately, and when Old Man refuses to disclose it Bero shoots him dead.

The patricide at the end of the play is the ultimate *dénouement* of the intense tension between the surface politeness and urbanity of the language of the play and the seething but repressed violence underneath it, as language itself becomes a double-edged sword, functioning both as the means of disclosing meaning as well as its concealment. It is the linguistic strategies of disguise that are the butt of satirical and ironic treatment in *Madmen and Specialists*. Indeed, the opening of the play reveals one such case of semantic repression, as the disabled Mendicants escape the reality of their disability by poking excessive fun at themselves in a game of dice in which they wager their remaining body parts:

AAFAA.   Three and two, born loser. What did you stake?
GOYI.   The stump of the left arm.
CRIPPLE.   Your last?
GOYI.   No, I have got one left.
BLINDMAN.   Your last. You lost the right stump to me yesterday.
GOYI.   Do you want it now or later?
BLINDMAN.   Keep it for now.

(SCP 2, 217)

The Mendicants' sense of humour is macabre, indicative of an extreme situation in which the dismemberment of the body or playing at it has become a suitable subject for and a device of the comic. Perhaps it affords the Mendicants a bit of comic relief from the incessant brutality of war, of which they are victims, but nevertheless its normalization of the abnormally cruel through the obliteration of the distinction between pain and laughter illustrates how, taken to the extreme, the idea of ethical relativity, a sound counterweight to dogmatism and fundamentalism, can itself be used to legitimize the wanton inversion of established ethical values on which the humane ideals of justice and social responsibility are predicated. Soyinka seems to be asking a very profound question here about the limits of moral relativity by demonstrating the malleability of the concept of the normal. Nevertheless, the Mendicants' witty verbal escapism occasionally allows a whiff of sadness to escape, indicating that there is a whole world of tortured feelings hidden away behind their language games.

Underneath the playful use of language there is, though, a distinct Juvenalian sternness, as their self-mockery is shown to mask an extremely amoral and ruthlessly calculating attitude to life. For example, the Mendicants are persuaded by Bero, for the promise of a fee, to spy on their teacher, Old Man, and we are given to understand that there is nothing in their concept of

41

morality that would make them think twice about betraying someone who has been as helpful to them as Old Man. In fact, the Mendicants are not an exception in this regard, as such an attitude is not only dominant in the society depicted in the play, but is also part and parcel of state ideology.

Bero's promise to look after the Mendicants makes them ready and willing to exchange one master for another. However, individualist and docile as the Mendicants are, one of them refuses to let Bero alone set the terms of their new job. Aafaa asserts his independence and tells Bero that, though the deal might be agreeable to his colleagues, he will not settle for something as vague as his promise of looking after them:

BERO.   I said, no more risks.
AAFAA.   That's for us to decide until you say how much... [*Bero cuts him across the face with his swagger stick. Aafaa staggers back, clutching the wound. Bero stands still watching him.*]

(SCP 2, 233)

Bero's violence towards Aafaa on account of the latter's rare candid expression of his views confirms how right the Mendicants are in being wary of using language as a means of communicating their true feelings about themselves and the world they inhabit, for in their society expressing oneself honestly is punishable. In addition the incident illustrates how, in a dictatorship, Hobson's choice is more of a norm than an exception, since the Mendicants are not really given a choice: they are only allowed to choose between the rebellious but doomed Old Man and the conforming son whose hold over them is inescapable: being disabled, they must depend on his medical expertise, just as for political survival they must rely on his power. They are thus aware that Old Man's choice, liberating as it is, is ultimately at the mercy of those who control the means of physical annihilation. No wonder that Aafaa never questions the Specialist again after having been beaten by him: he has learnt the limits of counter-identification with the state-sponsored ideology, for always the state's labour of interpellation is never too far away from its capacity to impose its will coercively, especially in a dictatorship such as is depicted in the play.

Perhaps we could argue that in *Madmen and Specialists* Soyinka shows that ideology is not only the means by which the subject is offered an imaginary view of his or her real relationship to social relations of production – as Louis Althusser suggests – but that it is also the realm of the symbolic enactment of the state's real coercive activity.[5] It may also be inferred from this that the very opposition between the interpellative and coercive functions of the state masks the extent of dialectical exchange between the two realms, which makes it additionally difficult to regard them as autonomous zones of state power. A good example of this is Bero, who is both the means of ideological interpellation and violent coercion, and whose presentation of such fusion is as witty and urbane as it is crude and menacing. This is true of the occasion when he reveals his cannibalism to the village priest and his sister:

BERO.　I give you the personal word of a scientist. Human flesh is delicious. Of course, not all parts of the body. I prefer the balls myself.

(*SCP* 2, 240)

Bero's refined language of the new African élite, practised, for example, by the Oguazors in *The Interpreters*, can be an ill-disguised sanitization of violence and evil. In this instance, language is once again employed as a site of concealment, exhibiting a dynamic tension between its form, the face it gives to the world, and its content – its character as the symbolization or inscription of political violence.

If the Mendicants use language as a form of escapism, in order to avoid facing up to the reality of their physical disability, Bero exemplifies how it can serve not only to disguise violence, but to embellish it and present it in the acceptable social idiom of a privileged linguistic register. Indeed, as he makes clear to his father, he considers himself part of an élite group, evil, but nevertheless exclusive. It is also revealing of the process of emotional disguise at work here that the manner in which Bero issues death threats to his father partakes of the sophisticated accent and inflection that would not be out of place at the Oguazor's cocktail parties, thus problematizing the relationship between class and oppressive rule. It is true that Idi Amin, crude in manner and untouched by the supposedly civilizing experience of a Western education, is very much seen as the quintessential African dictator. This simplification obviously makes the homburg-hatted, tuxedo-wearing Dr Banda and the sophisticated Francophile Mobuto Sese Seko conceal their violence in the specially selected mask of the discourse of Western civilization. As far as Soyinka is concerned, dictators are the same regardless of the language in which they choose to disguise their practice. It may also be noted in passing that Bero is similar to Tom Stoppard's President Mageba in *Night and Day*, whose training at Sandhurst, an élite British military academy, and at the London School of Economics, enhance his effectiveness as a dictator. There are larger issues here, which cannot be tackled in a short study, but suffice to say that one of the play's contributions to the study of power in Africa is its view that oppressive power does not conform to received ideas about barbarism and civilization.

It is the demythologization of the relationship between oppression and civilization to which Old Man is committed. Soyinka's Swiftian *reductio ad absurdum* is most explicit in Old Man's choice of cannibalism as part of his philosophy of As. As he recalls in a conversation with Bero:

> Oh, your faces gentlemen, your faces. You should see your faces. And your mouths hanging open. You are drooling, but I am not exactly sure why. Is there really much difference? All intelligent animals kill only for food, you know, and you are intelligent animals. Eat-eat-eat-eat-eat!

(SCP 2, 254)

Here we are presented with the barbarity of an uncritical pursuit of logic, which, as in the case of Lakunle's adoption of a shallow modernity in *The Lion and the Jewel*, is shown to erode the subtle and less precise aspects of human experience which are no less valuable for not being able to pass particular measures of scientific validity.

This is an understanding that is patently missing in Bero's application of scientific knowledge. He tells his father, 'To me you are simply another organism, another mould or strain under the lens. Sometimes a strain proves malignant and it becomes dangerous to continue with it. In such a case there is only one thing to do' (*SCP 2*, 262). Bero has reduced the complex signification of the human body to the singularity of biological discourse, thereby expunging ethics and morality from science;

and having done that, he can now torture humans with the precision afforded by his medical expertise without any moral compunction. In this respect, biological taxonomy, which is meant to increase our understanding of the complexity of relations among species, becomes the means by which human value itself is diminished. Soyinka is here alerting us to the dangers of forms of knowledge that have come to determine their validity internally rather than in terms of the broader context of social value. However, the debasement of scientific language in *Madmen and Specialists* is also a symptom of a larger crisis in the conception of power within the post-colonial society we are presented with in the play.

Power is defined in terms of the ability to establish absolute control, as Bero puts it bluntly to Old Man: 'I do not need illusions. I control lives' (*SCP 2*, 264). Yet the moral of the play is precisely that Bero's quest for absolute control is illusory, since Old Man has gone a step further than he and his colleagues could dare and proved to them that they are evil, and that their cruelty to others, ironically, does not depend on their transcendence of pain, but on their intense fear of it. Old Man is able not only to rehabilitate the victims of war physically, but to make them think differently about their world: and it is this that particularly worries Bero and the whole establishment, for, as he says: 'Father's assignment was to help the wounded readjust to the pieces and remnants of their bodies ... Instead he began to teach them to think' (*SCP 2*, 242). Old Man has not only taught them to think, but has also emancipated them from fear and, as Bero and the regime depend for their effectiveness on inspiring fear in the citizens, his philosophy has proved the limitations of their power and knowledge. It is the awareness of this that motivates Bero to have Old Man's secret at any cost. The more desperate he gets, the more difficult he finds it to conceal his violent desire behind his usual mask of sophistication:

> What exactly is As, Old Man? ... You know As, the playwork of your convalescents, the pivot of whatever doctrine you used to confuse their minds, your piffling battering ram at the idealism and purpose of this time and history. What is As, Old Man?

OLD MAN.   You seem to have described it to your satisfaction.

BERO.   [*Thundering. Moving suddenly, he passes his swagger stick across*

the Old Man's throat, holding it from behind and pressing.] I'm
asking you! What is As? Why As!

(*SCP* 2, 263)

He shoots his father for not revealing the key to As, but he has
not considered the availability of less obvious local forms of
resistance.

The earth mothers, the traditional herbalists who have been
helping his sister collect herbs for him, are displeased that,
contrary to tradition, they have unwittingly been co-opted into
Bero's murderous schemes. In anger they set fire to the house
while he is still in it. The destruction of Bero shows that there
are limits to the concealment of brutality through wit or
scientific rationality, and that there are always available less-
known, but equally powerful local idioms of power and
knowledge which, in their very marginality within the
contemporary post-colonial formation, offer a haunting remain-
der which ensures that power is not only what is constituted at
the centre by the dictators such as Bero or by radical, but equally
muddled philosophers such as Old Man.

The will to power disguised as a quest for emancipatory
knowledge receives further examination in Soyinka's *The Road*
(1965). With *Madmen and Specialists* and *A Dance of the Forests*, this
is one of the most metaphysical of Soyinka's works, as it
combines the existentialist concerns of *The Interpreters* and
Madmen and Specialists with the interest in the religious and
mythological aspects of identity of *A Dance of the Forests*. The
seriousness of the issues the play addresses can sometimes lead
to the mistaken view that it is wholly tragic. Yes, it is serious and
illustrates the tragedy of extreme hubris, but its distinctiveness
lies in the manner in which the tragic is blended with the comic.
Indeed, it is mainly through its satirical representation that the
play makes the important point that no social language is
exempt from being appropriated for authoritarian purposes.

Professor, like Old Man in *Madmen and Specialists*, and in some
ways like Kongi in *Kongi's Harvest*, is engaged in a quest for a
general philosophical system. He is looking for what he terms
the 'Word', which is never really explained in the text, but is
understood to refer to something akin to the key to life.
However, unlike Old Man, whose philosophy of As is used to
undermine oppressive rule, Professor's quest is, as Bero's, a

means to power. Even so, his first appearance on stage is as comic as Lakunle's in *The Lion and the Jewel*; he is described as:

> A tall figure in Victorian outfit – tails, top hat etc., all thread-bare and shiny at the lapels from much ironing. He carries four enormous bundles of newspapers and a fifth of paper odds and ends impaled on a metal rod stuck in a wooden rest. A chair-stick hangs from one elbow, and the other arm clutches a road-sign bearing a squiggle and the one word, 'Bend'.

(SCP 1, 156–7)

In fact, Professor has just returned from one of his trips searching for the Word, and the only word he has found is a signpost he has just uprooted from the road, endangering road users. However, given that he is also the proud owner of the so-called AKSIDENT STORE, the removal of the signpost can be seen as a way of increasing the speed with which his shop may be supplied with new stock.

Also, his excessive rhetorical flights show someone trying too hard to sound profound and mystical:

> PROF.   *[he enters in a high state of excitement, muttering to himself.]* ... In this dawn has exceeded its promise. A new discovery every hour – I am used to that, but that I should be led to where this was hidden, sprouted in secret for heaven knows how long... for there was no doubt about it, this word was growing, it was growing from earth until I plucked it...

(SCP 1, 157)

As the speech bathetically moves from the exalted religious register to the assertion that the road sign is a secret outgrowth of the Word one begins to wonder whether the word 'bend' is not in fact metonymically referring to the possibility that Professor himself may have gone round the bend. Mad or not, the episode reveals the inhumanity of his project, which is most spectacularly exhibited in his privileging of the search over truth itself and other concerns, including road safety and respect for the dead. Like Bero, he subordinates everything to his pursuit of power and knowledge. For instance, he seems to take enormous pleasure in watching a car accident by the bend from where he later removes the signpost, concentrating more on the possibility of the event revealing some aspect of the 'elusive Word' than on its tragic import.

Like that of Soyinka's interpreters, Professor's effort to fashion a new philosophical and religious system does not lead to a greater understanding of his world, but rather to more confusion even over the meaning of the most ordinary objects and words. Clearly, when a philosophical system leads someone like Professor to read serious philosophical meaning in road signs then something is obviously amiss. The main difficulty with his quest is that he has erased the distinction between the two levels of semantic signification: the literal and figurative, and further, for the mystical pleasure it gives him and the monopoly it affords him over the key to meaning, privileged the latter over the former. Another example of this can be gleaned from his indiscriminate use in ordinary conversation of the serious tone and expression associated with the religious and the oracular. However, Professor's residence in the stratosphere of the language of religious experience is not altruistic, for it also invests him with power over those around him, especially the inhabitants of the roadside shack, over whom he presides like a Colossus, so to speak.

With the difference between the two realms of reference abolished, the Professor can arrogate to himself what Derek Walcott, in a radically different context, has termed the 'Adamic power' to name anew.[6] He can start afresh reinventing a whole new language in which objects are renamed in terms of his own idiolect rather than in those of a shared and publicly available discourse of meaning. It is this subversion of the normal reference points that forms the basis of Professor's control of the interpretive resources of the universe of the play, as the erasure of the boundary between the two realms of meaning creates a gap through which he is able to slot a private rather than public view of the arbitrary relations between signs and their corresponding referents.

It is equally in this respect that his pretensions to superhuman identity become obvious, as his obsession with the Word, with all its biblical association, such as 'in the beginning was the Word, and the Word was God', reveals itself as a desire to create a symbolic system in which he himself becomes the sole source of the meaning of the Word, and, equally, its living manifestation. (St. John's 1: 1) Thus, in Professor, Soyinka offers an example of an extremely subtle appropriation of Christianity, less obvious than Jero's explicitly mercenary use, but nevertheless similarly parasitic. Brenda Cooper has described Professor as a false Ogun; we could add that he is also a false Christ, a sort of double negation of both the indigenous and received religious traditions.[7] The Word then, when it is to be revealed, is likely to be stamped with the eccentric syncretism of Professor's quest for it.

Professor's expulsion from the Church for locking horns with his Bishop indicates his inability to accept being led by others and his expectation that he has to be the leader in every circumstance, even when he has not been formally inducted in particular rituals of leadership. Indeed, when he is thrown out of the Church and decides to keep watch over it from its permanent source of torment, the roadside shack opposite, he takes his leadership of the roadside dwellers as a matter of course, oblivious to the fact that they may have their own criteria for such positions. His inability to grasp this truth in the end precipitates his downfall as, similar to his experience in the Church, he is cast away, in a manner of speaking, from the fellowship of the shack-dwellers.

Initially, Professor's religious and philosophical pretensions win him admiration among the roadside dwellers, who find the gravitas of his bearing and his preoccupation with the mysterious Word self-evidently worthy of leadership and adoration. Indeed, his quest for the Word helpfully, as far as the aspiring drivers are concerned, still leaves him with enough time to forge driving and vehicle licences, and his handwork is well known to traffic policemen such as the corrupt Particular Joe, whose name itself testifies to his inordinate interest in particulars of travellers for the sole purpose of extorting money from them. In this context it can be argued that Professor's quest for the Word is perhaps as much a counterfeit as the documents he forges and that, like his documents, the credibility of his religious and philosophical practice will depend less on its intrinsic value and more on its material profitability to himself and his followers. He is useful in other practical ways, for he runs a shop for second-hand car spares. Again, it is difficult to take his religious concerns seriously when we are told that he specializes in spare parts cannibalized from cars freshly involved in accidents, and we are additionally informed that his appetite for car parts is so intense that, at times, cars have been brought in for dismantling with dead bodies still in them. Professor's business can also be read as an apt metaphor for his quest, which is also based on recycling odds and ends culled from a variety of sources.

Nevertheless, even though his practical favours for the shack-dwellers get him some support, behind his back they regard him as either a madman or a dangerous meddler in things he knows nothing about. This is especially true of Say Tokyo, the self-Americanized gangster, who does not mind drinking Professor's evensong palm-wine but finds his use of traditional religious practice unnerving and provocative. Professor's encroachment on traditional belief begins with his adoption of the road as a personal symbol, transferring it from its location in the communal system of cosmological representation to his own semiotic idiolect. The road is a multiple sign in traditional Yoruba metaphysics: it is where Ogun, the god of iron, lies in wait for unsuspecting travellers to consume them or the substitute propitiatory sacrifice of a dog. It is also the point of ontological duality, as it represents both the world of the living and the dead, a space in which travellers coexist with the spirits of their dead predecessors. Above all, the road also serves as a point of transition, a liminal space, between the plane of the gods, that of the living, and that of the dead. In short, in Soyinka's mythopoesis, the road is a heterogeneous site of a dynamic interplay and exchange between distinct, but yet overlapping modalities of being. Thus Professor's appropriation of such a rich source of communal meaning for a personal quest enacts, in the realm of cultural capital, the mechanics of private accumulation of the means of production that Soyinka has dramatized in, for example, *Opera Wonyosi*, as well as his most recent play, *The Beatification of Area Boy: A Lagosian Kaleidoscope* (1995). The idea of the road is central to Soyinka's mythopoesis and politics: it features in his early poems in *Idanre and Other Poems*, just as it also became a point of focus for his public attempts in the seventies and eighties to contribute to the reduction of road accidents on Nigerian roads.

However, in the play, he reminds us that the meaning of the road, as that of any word, is mediated by ideological interest and the specific site of local signification in which it is situated. Nevertheless, he is equally concerned to point out that it is not only language that is at stake in Professor's parasitic symbolic mediation of the road, but larger cultural symbols as well. Equally abused are the rituals of Ogun's worship: the ritualistic consumption of palm-wine and the egungun masquerade dance, for instance.[8] Since palm-wine-tappers are servants of Ogun, by virtue of working with iron, Professor's adoption of Murano as a personal tapper is an example of a self-arrogation of divine power that comes near the Christian idea of blasphemy. This is more so as Murano's Agemo state, half-human and half-spirit, accentuates his links with the super-natural, putting Professor in the position of a mortal whose desire for power makes him turn a divinity, semi-divine perhaps, but nevertheless someone evidently of the realm of the spirits, into a personal slave.

Even more subversive of traditional religion is Professor's preservation of Murano for his quest, as Murano is subjected to the same interpretive strategies as employed in determining the spiritual significance of the word 'bend'. Professor considers him the repository of the Word. Yet, his identification of Murano with a god is based on some obviously dubious interpretation:

SAMSON.   . . . But his legs are the same.
PROF.   Blind!
KOTONU.   Oh I admit he limps. He seems okay to me.
PROF.   When a man has one leg in each world, his legs are never the same. The big toe of Murano's foot – the left one of course – rests on the slumbering chrysalis of the Word. When that crust cracks my friends – you and I, that is the moment we await. That is the moment of rehabilitation.

(SCP 1, 186–7).

There is also a strong suggestion here that Professor may violently extract the Word out of Murano should he deem that the moment has arrived for the Word to be made visible.

Indeed, that is what happens in the play, as Professor in a moment of inebriation forces Murano to re-enact the Egungun ritual, in the middle of which he had previously had an accident; and as Professor conjures spirits, Say Tokyo, the Americanized gangster, kills him and is in turn smashed by the masked Egungun. Say Tokyo's intervention in Professor's appropriation of the language of tradition for personal use suggests that despite his Americanized identity, which could be seen as a sign of alienation, he is still at heart more grounded in the traditions of his people than Professor. It is true that they both fashion hybrid identities for purposes of using such difference in order to wield power over others. Professor's religious and philosophical syncretism, as has been shown, is meant solely to feed his megalomania, and it is also evident that Say Tokyo's Americanism is merely a way of asserting an authentic gangster identity, making him revered by other gangsters as well as his customers, such as the politician who gives him the job of attacking political opponents. In the end, though, the two forms of functional hybridity differ in the extent to which they tamper with the foundations of tradition.

It is however significant that Soyinka makes Say Tokyo, a political thug, the defender of African cultural authenticity in the play. It shows that the concern with the preservation of African culture is not just the monopoly of the learned and distinguished – if at all, Professor is a good example of that – but is also something that ordinary people such as the tramps and other dwellers of the roadside regard as extremely important. Moreover, it also suggests that the project of cultural conservation may not always be underpinned by the most progressive politics, for the sort of political company Say Tokyo keeps is certainly more in the nature of Kongi and Kamini than, for instance, Daodu or Segi.

Ultimately, the tragic dimension of the play, like its comedy, lies in the manner in which Professor fools himself more than anyone else about the validity of his quest. As his playful performance of the imaginary real intermingles with the reality of religious practice, the tension between the surface rhetorical presentation of his quest and its disguised violence erupts to the surface, foregrounding the tragic content of comedy. It is this transcendence of the distinction between the two genres that Soyinka excels in in the texts examined in this chapter, always attempting to explore new possibilities of dissolving the boundary between the genres and reconstituting them as fluid zones of generic identity exchange. Nevertheless, he is also a purist, as we saw in the previous chapter and as will be shown again in relation to tragedy in the next.

4

Redemptive Tragedies

Tragedy is Soyinka's primary love, for it offers him a language in which he is able to fuse together imperceptibly his interest in the metaphysical and mythological with his broader political concerns. Yet, even here one notices that his approach ranges from the purity of the Aristotelian paradigm to that of traditional African modes of the tragic. There are also several works which have a sustained solemnity of mood, characterization, and action and which, as his tragedies, dwell on the agony of African post-colonial existence, but which nevertheless only fit in in conventional as well as in Soyinka's own syncretic notions of tragedy with the greatest difficulty. Such texts have the grim pessimism of *The Interpreters* without its satire and irony, very much representing the diremption of the tension between the satiric and the tragic we saw in *Madmen and Specialists* and *The Road* into a singularly unrelieved, anguished reflection on the nature of social and political evil.

This is best exemplified by Soyinka's *A Dance of the Forests* (1963), which was produced for the celebrations of Nigeria's independence from Britain in 1960. The play dramatizes the tragic quality of African history and mythology in order to make a statement about the future, not only of Nigeria, but of post-colonial Africa in general. Soyinka reports that when he was a student he met some of the leaders-in-waiting of post-colonial Nigeria and, listening to them, he realized that in a curious way the post-colonial was a repetition of certain historical abuses of power; and it is this iterative nature of power that is the subject of *A Dance of the Forests*.[1]

The play tells a story of how the inhabitants of a certain post-colonial African town decide to invite ancestral spirits from the Forest of the Dead to a celebratory gathering of the tribes, where they also hope to find out from the ancestors what the future holds for them. However, human vanity is such that they only desire the company of important and pristine spirits, but the dead who turn up are not exactly palatable to the eye, as they seem to have just got up from their graves. It is decided that the horrible apparitions must be driven back and, in case Forest Head sends more, they set fire to the forest in order to keep all spirits at bay. Nevertheless, by this time, Forest Head himself has already arrived and is disguised in human form. He entices Demoke, the son of the head of the council, and others into the Forest of the Dead; and their fate, particularly Demoke's, is dependent on Forest Head's dexterity of arbitration among human-like squabbling spirits and deities. When they finally come back to the world of the living, they are not able to offer any meaningful statement as to what the gods and the ancestors have in store for humanity. From their behaviour, though, it appears that the gods may not themselves have a better view of the future than humanity. However, in between all this we are presented with a dramatization of the dead ancestors's own past which is also that of the reincarnated post-colonial inhabitants.

What is revealed is a complex illustration of how the past is paradigmatic of the present endless reproducibility and universality of evil. In the pre-colonial African monarch, Mata Kharibu, we have an example of a leader without any scruples and whose sole concern, like that of the post-colonial leadership of Kongi and Kamini, is with self-aggrandizement and absolute power. Kharibu takes the wife of a neighbouring King, Madame Tortoise (Rola in post-colonial times), for a lover; and when the husband does not react as he expects, he and Madame Tortoise, both of whom are extremely keen on a fight for the sheer love of violence, cast around for a pretext on which to invade the neighbouring Kingdom. In the end, some flimsy excuse is found, but, to the King's and Madame Tortoise's surprise, the General refuses to fight what he regards as an unjust war. Madame Tortoise, having failed to persuade him to change his mind with the offer of her body, falsely accuses him of attempted rape and has him castrated and sold into slavery and his pregnant wife murdered. As it turns out, the General and his wife are the deformed dead spirits that have been sent to represent the ancestral spirits at the gathering of the tribes.

It is not only the King and the Queen who mete out extreme violence in the pre-colonial kingdom depicted in the play: others are equally evil. There is the Court Poet (reincarnated as Demoke, the carver), who pushes his assistant to death because of his jealousy over Madame Tortoise's preferring the young assistant to him. The poet's action is repeated in the post-colonial times, when Demoke also causes the death of his apprentice while cutting down the sacred Oro tree for carving what is described as 'a symbol of the great reunion' of the tribes. Overall, evil is presented as transhistorical, as we see it being reproduced in the present post-colonial formation through the reincarnation of the past as both subjectivity and event. Here, Soyinka seems to be arguing that the present is not different from the past, since there is no radical break between the two in terms of the nature of private as well as public social and political relations.

Thus, as far as the playwright is concerned, the end of colonial oppression may not necessarily lead to the eradication of oppression in general. This message may have seemed a little too pessimistic, perhaps, on the eve of a nation's founding moment in 1960, but in retrospect it is hardly so, being instead an accurate prediction of the Nigerian post-colonial experience as well as that of the majority of African countries. Indeed, as portrayed in *A Dance of the Forests*, evil seems to be a fundamentally entrenched aspect of human history: the court historian, seeking to provide his master with the expected justification for waging war against Madame Tortoise's husband, cynically argues that war and violence are in fact the only motor of human history, asking, 'Would Troy, if it were standing today, lay claim to preservation in the annals of history if a thousand valiant Greeks had not been slaughtered before its gates, and a hundred thousand Trojans within her walls?' (*SCP 1*, 51)

Soyinka's universalization of evil is not an attempt to rationalize the failings of pre-colonial Africa, but rather a subtle way of avoiding falling into the trap of the logic of what Abdul JanMohamed, in his book *Manichean Aesthetics* (1983), calls the 'Manichean dichotomy', that is, the idea underlying the representation of Africa in colonial discourse in which the African continent and its people are portrayed as embodying an essential barbarism that is in absolute opposition to an inherently civilized Europe. In many ways the notion of Manichean dichotomy is an extension of Edward Said's critique of Western Orientalist discourse presented in *Orientalism* (1978). It is a mark of Soyinka's dexterity that, while candidly recovering the African past, warts and all, he simultaneously forestalls the possibility of his work being co-opted into ideological projects whose objectives are radically opposed to his, particularly racist constructions of the continent. There is also a more immediate reason for globalizing the context of corrupt power in Mata Kharibu's Kingdom. The play is set in the period of the transatlantic slave trade and, indeed, includes an episode on slave trading in which the Court Physician and the Slave Dealer have a witty and refined chat about the business of selling humans. The slave trade is also seen to serve the needs of despotic rule well: as exemplified by the fate of the General, it provides the most effective way of getting rid of the opposition. In this way, the exile of the opposition in post-colonial Africa may be regarded as being in the same category as the diaspora occasioned by the slave trade: whereas pre-colonial dictators may simply have sold the opposition into slavery, the post-colonial ones create conditions which achieve similar population drainage. This, however, is not to suggest that the experience of post-colonial exile is in any measure equivalent to the horror of the slave trade.

Nevertheless, it may be argued, as a number of critics have, that in *A Dance of the Forests* Soyinka uses a cyclic notion of history which does not allow for the idea of radical difference between the past and the present and that this concept of cyclicity constitutes a pessimistic rather than optimistic view of the future of post-colonial Africa. Soyinka would himself not disagree with such an assessment of the play, but would perhaps only add that what is important is not whether or not it is pessimistic, but the contribution of such a representation to the critical examination of the role of the past in the process of constructing a post-colonial future. In a context in which the celebration of the African past has been abused by dictators such as Mobuto Sese Seko and others, it is vital that one retrieves not only a generalized version of the African past, but also one that shows its tragic mistakes. In addition to the general critique of slavery offered in the play, something that also concerns Soyinka greatly is how to make sense of African participation in such an abominable practice. It is obviously a complex matter involving a variety of factors, but even so, Soyinka would suggest that we learn to take responsibility not only for the celebrated feats of the past, Sundiata's and Chaka's statesmanship, or the various forms of indigenous technological development, for example, but also for the history of the abuse of power. It is here that he performs what he considers to be the essential role of the African writer, that is acting as the conscience of his society rather than its hypocritical praise-singer.

Pessimistic as the play is, there is a glimmer of hope as we are shown that, regardless of the difficulties involved in fighting against tyranny, history also offers the example of Kharibu's general who is able to say no even on pain of death. He serves as an example of the kind of redemptive leadership in the course of which the whole society is renewed, an embodiment of Soyinka's tragic ideal exemplified by such protagonists as Eman in *The Strong Breed* and Ofeyi and Iriyise in *Season of Anomy*. Also, the conflict between the general and his master provides Soyinka with the opportunity to bring in aspects of Greek tragedy, such as *hubris* and *hamartia* (tragic error of judgement). Mata Kharibu finds this rare gesture of opposition troubling and, his Soothsayer's observations are not reassuring either, as all he tells him is, 'I see much blood ... on both sides of the plough' (*SCP 1*, 52). But foolishly, Kharibu says, 'I will be satisfied with that. Does it not mean a great battle?' (*SCP 1*, 52) Thus he makes an error of judgement which in the end leads to his downfall. Additionally, the King is shown to be consumed with *hubris*, a flaw in many a classical tragic hero, including Sophocles' Oedipus. However, beyond this, Soyinka does not draw much on the Aristotelian concept of tragedy in this play, relying instead for its structure on a cinematic alternation between past and present as well as between the world of the living and that of the dead.

The inclusion of the dead in what is essentially a comparison between the past and the present introduces an element that complicates both the structure and theme of the play. Structurally the frame of the Forest dwellers is predominantly a dramatization of Yoruba cosmology, delivered through traditional dance and mime; and, as such, it shows Soyinka exploring the theatrical value of elements of traditional African culture. It also forms a surrealistic contrast to the realism of the historical world of Mata Kharibu as well as that of the post-colonial present. However, in terms of the particular plotting of time in the play, the Forest is also the teleological terminus of the past, as it contains most of the dead that would have formed part of the pre-colonial past inhabited by Mata Kharibu. Also within the context of traditional African ancestral worship, in which it is believed that the dead co-exist with the living, the Forest dwellers are co-present with the post-colonial space and, indeed, inhabit it; and they have the capacity either to harm or enhance it.

The adaptation of traditional African cosmology and pre-colonial African as well as European history to the needs of a distinctly post-colonial critique which we see in the play testifies, again, to Soyinka's determination to use the totality of his intellectual and cultural heritage, African and European, as a resource for fashioning a distinct post-colonial political peda-gogy. The play also shows an imaginative use of a wide range of theatrical idioms, convincingly illustrating the writer's ability to delve beneath the surface of the contemporary post-colonial formation so as to highlight, among other things, the problem-atic nature of the African past, subjecting it to the same ruthless interrogation that he applies to his critique of the colonial past as well as the post-colonial present.

Soyinka continues his double-edged critique in *The Swamp Dwellers* (1963), another play which he wrote while a student in Britain and which was first performed in 1959 as part of the *Sunday Times* Student Festival. As Eldred Durosimi Jones rightly notes, it is a 'graver' play than *The Lion and the Jewel*, written at the same time.[3] If the latter demonstrates Soyinka's mastery of satire, *The Swamp Dwellers* reveals his ability to present an intensely emotive situation within a very short space of dramatic time. It is much shorter than *A Dance of the Forests* and its thematic and temporal scope are more limited: it is set in a village and uses simple chronological time rather than the complex form of *A Dance of the Forests*. Its main focus is the erosion of traditional values and the consequent loss of hope among the young generation, as they are left with very few cultural and moral reference points with which to shore up their precarious inhabitation of the modern world.

In the play, Igwezu, a young man from the country, joins his twin brother in the city to try and avail himself of the economic opportunities the city is supposed to offer. However, when he gets there his wife runs off with his brother, who is well-adapted to the new place and its ways. Furthermore, when he is short of money, he borrows some from the brother, putting up the expected harvest from his piece of land in the village as security for the loan. To his disappointment, when he goes home he finds the crop washed away by floods. When he seeks a consoling explanation from the spiritual and political leader of the village, to whom he had offered the required sacrifice before leaving for the city, the Kadiye asks for more money. In anger, Igwezu almost murders him and he has to flee the village in fear of the Priest's vengeance. He leaves behind, though, a blind beggar from the drought-stricken North who has come down to the marshland in the hope of succour, but who finds that here it is the overabundance of water rather than its shortage that is the problem. Nevertheless, he promises to keep an eye on things for Igwezu while he is away.

There is no room for hope in the play, as the whole country seems to suffer from natural disasters and even in places like the city, where nature is not so capricious, there are socially produced sources of deprivation which rob someone like Igwezu of even imagining his personal and community's fortunes changing for the better. He belongs to a generation which can look neither to tradition nor to the modernity offered by the African city for ethical moorings, since both are being mediated by greed and a rapacious materialism in a way that is not dissimilar to the general ruthlessness of Mata Kharibu's kingdom. Thus, once again, Soyinka cautions against taking tradition at its face value and regarding its self-presentation as an uncontaminated repository of the nation's moral purity as objectively true.

Equally, the city's materialism is presented as threatening the personal and social links which had once been valued and useful in the village, but now it is everyone for himself, and even institutions such as marriage are suitably adapted to fit in with the new times. Igwezu is thus in no-man's land, an in-between figure who finally leaves his village without any clue as to where he is going and what the future will bring for him and his community. He is an angry young man, but in a situation where the resources with which to translate that anger into a constructive alternative are markedly absent. So at the end of the play, when he marches off into the dark, angry and despondent, he grows into a symbol not only of his generation of the deprived, but also of all those who, in the furious interplay between tradition and modernity in the post-colonial moment, find themselves outside both spaces, without plenitude in either.

However, it is in its particular attention to the question of the rebellion of the youth against adult authority that *The Swamp Dwellers* resembles Soyinka's 1965 radio play, *Camwood on the Leaves* (1965), in which a father's violent treatment of his son drives the latter to patricide. In both plays, Soyinka is interrogating a fundamental African belief that elders should be respected and that they are a source of wisdom. Evidently, the sample of elders presented in the two plays shows that this aspect of tradition is oblivious to the possibility of its being colonized, so to speak, by other, even exploitative values. The village priest of *The Swamp Dwellers* is as keen as Reverend Erinjobi of *Camwood on the Leaves* to use the expectation that the young should respect the elders to oppress them.

As the two represent not only adult, but also religious authority, the object of criticism in the two plays, is the corrupt religious leadership, both African and Western, which employs religion as an instrument of oppression. Nevertheless, there is a marked difference between the responses of the protagonists of these two plays to tyranny: Igwezu flees, but Isola kills his tormentor, suggesting, in the first case, the youth's helplessness, with withdrawal being the only choice left for him, and in the second, the protagonist's active intervention in his fate which reverses the power relations between the oppressor and the oppressed, but which also, tragically, leads to the death of the father. In this context, then, *Camwood on the Leaves* is more tragic than *The Swamp Dwellers*, where nothing more catastrophic happens to the protagonist than his departure from the village. It is, however, the pervading sense of being trapped in an overwhelmingly oppressive social and political situation that links these two plays to Soyinka's prison poems, *A Shuttle in the*

Crypt (1972), in which the conflict between the individual and state leads to the deprivation of personal freedom.

Between 1967 and 1969 Soyinka was detained by the Nigerian authorities; and his crime was to have tried to stop the supply of arms to both the Federal Government and the seceding Republic of Biafra. More than that, he went to the predominantly Moslem North and also crossed to Biafra to see if he could find a way of stopping the war and forging new alliances that went beyond identification with one's ethnic or religious group. Upon his return, he was arrested and kept in prison for two years. Soyinka has presented this painful period of his life in his prison memoirs, *The Man Died* (1972). However, in *A Shuttle in the Crypt*, he is able to employ the wide range of narrative devices that poetry affords him to attend to the subtle and intimate ways in which the experience of imprisonment inscribed itself on his mind.

The imprisoned poet imagines himself as a shuttle, but a shuttle conceived of as 'a unique species of caged animal, restless bolt of energy, trapped weaver bird yet charged in repose with unspoken forms and designs' (*SC* vii). This poetic conceit, as he describes it, becomes the means by which he protects himself from the 'inhuman isolation' of prison life. Self-protection is necessary, for others less well prepared have succumbed to the mental destruction engendered by confinement, as we see in 'To the Madmen over the Wall', where the poet laments the mental condition of fellow prisoners in a neighbouring cell:

> Howl, howl
> Your fill and overripeness of the heart,
> I may not come with you
> Companions of the broken buoy
> I may not seek
> The harbour of your drifting shore.

> (*SC* 18)

There is a deep empathy with their plight, even though, clearly, the poet would rather not join them on their 'drifting shore'. He is a shuttle that must escape the fate of the howling companions by keeping moving constantly. Even so, he sees in the loud expression of anguish of his neighbours an important way of conveying to their captors the frailty of the human body, as he says:

> Closer I not come
> But though I set my ears against
> The tune of setting forth, yet, howl
> Upon the hour of sleep, tell these walls
> The human heart may hold
> Only so much despair.

(*SC* 18)

He has not himself escaped it altogether, as he howls involuntarily in his sleep, indicating that the madmen are not wholly exceptional, but merely a more obvious expression of the mental strain under which every mind, including the persona's labours in this inhuman habitation. Thus in time, they may all, the shuttle and others, drift towards the shore of the howlers.

Yet, there are moments in the anthology when the poet is able to celebrate snatches of hope. In 'Ujamaa', a poem dedicated to the former president of Tanzania and his ideology of African Socialism, it is clear that, regardless of the suffering inflicted on the poet by his country's leadership, such a situation is not universally true of the continent, and that somewhere his political vision would not only find an echo, but a whole validating political philosophy and practice. Equally, towards the end of the anthology we are offered an elegy to the late Nigerian poet Christopher Okigbo and others whom the persona considers exemplary of inspiring leadership both in life and death. Likewise, in *Mandela's Earth* (1989) and *Ogun Abibiman* (1976), the poet celebrates the lives and suffering of Winnie and Nelson Mandela.

Transformative agency is very much conceptualized in terms of the primal rebellion of the godhead's slave, Atunda, who rolled a boulder over him and so splintered his divine essence, giving rise to the many Yoruba deities. In *Idanre and Other Poems* (1967), Atunda is praised thus: 'All hail Saint Atunda, First revolutionary | Grand Iconoclast at genesis' (*IOP* 83), presenting his dismemberment of divine hegemony into multiple divine forms as paradigmatic of a universal revolutionary agency. Soyinka's compatriot and fellow poet, Niyi Osundare, defines the Atunda ideal as a 'creative and re-creative, iconoclastic, rebellious, libertarian and frequently revolutionary, an instant, almost natural, opposition to "constituted authority" especially the inhuman, totalitarian kind ... A subversive, transgressive spirit in constant argument with customary "givens" '. (Maja-Pearce 83)

A more elaborate presentation of the Atunda ideal is to be found in Soyinka's epic novel, *Season of Anomy*, where Ofeyi, the youthful marketing manager of a powerful business corporation known as the Cartel, and his girlfriend Iriyise, a dancer in the company's cocoa promotion troupe, team up to undermine the Cartel's effort to incorporate into its cocoa product market a newly discovered village which, having been bypassed by history, as it were, has preserved a communalist political and economic practice that is diametrically opposed to the exploitative system out of which the Cartel has emerged and which it now defends with both money and arms. The village decides to resist by extending its own underground network to most of the country and even to the national armed forces. The network has always been there as a vehicle for diffusing life-enhancing values to the larger society. As Ofeyi assumes the leadership of the movement and begins to interfere with the Cartel's propaganda machine, the Cartel kidnaps Iriyise and hides her away in a mental asylum, which it is hoped will persuade him not to go further with his scheme. However, the opposite happens, as this makes him more determined than ever to oppose the Cartel more methodically. He and his Americanized jazz-player friend Zaccheus embark on a hazardous search for Iriyise, and in their travels come across scenes of carnage perpetrated by the Cartel, as every manner of difference, including ethnicity and religion, is used as an excuse to attack anyone suspected of not accepting its authority. He finally retrieves Iriyise, but he and his movement, as happens to Daodu and Segi in *Kongi's Harvest*, fail to destroy the Cartel, though one is left with the impression that they will try again.

The novel should be seen as an imaginative rendering in prose of Soyinka's experiences just before and during his imprisonment and, as such, it mines the same vein as *The Man Died* and *A Shuttle in the Crypt*.[3] What *Season of Anomy* has in common with the two texts is a concern with grasping the details of the operations of oppressive power in the day-to-day functioning of public institutions as well as how such a process impinges on the lives of citizens. Moreover, the novel also articulates the writer's belief in the possibility of such power being undermined and superseded by other forms of political practice. In Ofeyi's redemptive labour, the novel re-enacts the structure of traditional Yoruba regenerative agency offered in the ritual of Ogun's primordial transgression of the abyss of separation between the gods and humanity.

We are shown the necessity of strong and inspirational leadership in the pursuit of counter-hegemonic politics, but such agency is not conceived of in essentialist terms; rather, it is shown to be engendered by a sensitivity to a collective desire for change glimpsed beneath the surface display of support for authoritarian rule. It is thus a matter of reading the signs, determining the moment when discontent is not just a product of the mechanics of oppression, but the stirring of an urge for purposeful transformation. Furthermore, it is shown that the implementation of the Atunda ideal or the Ogunian transgression is only efficacious if grounded in a set of shared nurturing values. Ofeyi relies on old Ahime as much as Aiyero does on him; wherever he goes he is helped by members of the Aiyero underground network or others who are just against injustice and welcome the opportunity to do something about it. It is in this respect that critics who accuse Soyinka of presenting solitary individuals as agents of change can be described as failing to appreciate the complexity of his conceptualization of counter-hegemonic agency.

In the end though, it is the protagonist's choice that determines his or her agency. The process involves a clear counter-identification with dominant ideology and a decisive embracing of an oppositional set of values. This is what Ofeyi does in the novel. He rejects a number of offers from the Cartel when its members become aware of his unhappiness at their attempts to enmesh the people of Aiyero into their web. He also has the chance of marrying into the family of one of the most influential members of the Cartel, but he rejects all this for the sake of helping the village of Aiyero and the values it represents. This is true of Iriyise, too, who gives up singing songs promoting the Cartel's products and adopts those which teach people about the Cartel's iniquitous activities. In the example of these two characters and others in the novel, Soyinka shows transformative agency as primarily involving a clear sense of counter-identification with a hegemonic ideology and the cultivation of an alternative political praxis.

It is a mark of supreme subversion that Ofeyi's radical agency inhabits the very body of hegemonic rule, invasively using it against itself and for the propagation of the counter-politics of Aiyero's communalism. As he explains:

> The idea that came from his first encounter with the commune was only one of many that sought to retrieve his occupation from its shallow world of jingles and the greater debasement of exploitation by the Cartel. The pattern could be reversed, the trick of conversion applied equally to the Cartel's technical facilities...Ofeyi envisioned the parallel progress of the new idea, the birth of the new man from the same germ as the cocoa seed, the Aiyero ideal disseminated with the same powerful propaganda machine of the Cartel throughout the land. (*SA* 253)

His method is not one of breaking apart the godhead of power, as in the case of Atunda, a direct frontal approach, but rather of subterranean location of counter-agency and of employing such a position to infuse the host with new political marrow, in the hope that in due course its overall content will be transformed into the new ideology.[4] Having decided on this course of action, Ofeyi requires an Ogunian willpower to traverse the realm between desire and plenitude.

One of the issues he must resolve is whether he would authorize the use of force against the regime if his gradualist politics were met by state violence. Iriyise's capture begins to make him wonder whether he had been right in discounting such a possibility. The Dentist, a sort of Che Guevara figure, is in no doubt whatsoever that state violence must be met by the masses' counter-violence, but Ofeyi had not been so certain that was the best way forward. Now, however, faced with the possible death of someone close to him, and also with the possible massacre of his supporters, he is slowly beginning to change his views on the matter, showing the difficulty of reconciling the personal and the public in the pursuit of a political cause. Eventually, he is forced by events to pick up a gun and shoot dead one of the government agents attempting to kill a besieged civil servant whose only crime is that he comes from the wrong ethnic group.

Season of Anomy also shows the importance of the totality of the experience of struggle for the regeneration of the community. Although the Aiyero ideal is never fully established in the rest of the country by the end of the novel, and though it is clear that the state is going to fight to death in order to safeguard its privileges, the process of communal resistance, even though its results are not tangible, is seen as renewing the strength of all who have participated in it. Thus, much as there is no change in the balance of power between the oppressors and the oppressed, the latter have nevertheless gained in the knowledge that they need not suffer quietly and that they are a large and diverse group which still has a chance of overcoming the forces of tyranny. So, to the extent that the success of a given elaboration of the Atunda or Ogunian agency is its capacity to transform political consciousness, it is not just an individualist project, but a fundamentally communal one. It is in this regard that Soyinka is sometimes regarded as socialist; and he is, but, of course, not in the doctrinaire way in which Socialism and Marxism are publicly articulated in Africa. Since Soyinka's is contaminated with the metaphysics of agency based on paradigms of transformation taken from ritual and tragedy, it cannot be considered scientific, but that, so Soyinka would argue, does not make it any less valid as a mode of apprehending and modifying hegemonic ideologies of post-colonial formation. In short, he puts a great premium on the idea that the suffering of an individual for a social good may renew not himself alone, but his or her whole community as well. Indeed, for him, tragedy is the supreme arena of such transformative suffering.

This reconceptualization of tragedy is best exemplified by Soyinka's adaptation of Euripides' classical play, *The Bacchae*, to which title he significantly adds the phrase 'a communion ritual'. Commissioned by the National Theatre in London, Soyinka's *The Bacchae of Euripides* was first performed by the company in 1973 at the Old Vic. The play, which Soyinka had studied as an undergraduate student at the University of Ibadan, must have been one of the early texts that introduced him to ancient Greek writing and culture which have provided him with an important cultural resource in terms of which and, perhaps, also against which to rethink and elaborate Yoruba cosmology into a modern African poetics of tragedy. First and foremost, Soyinka's reworking of the play does away with its original theme of revenge, as the characterization of the protagonists and the action and its motivation as well as the setting are modified so that the conventional world of Greek tragedy is infused with elements of African cosmology and ritual as well as Soyinka's own particular politics of commitment.

He rewrites the discourse of Classical tragedy by transforming the original Greek dramatic categories, such as pity and fear, in such a way that they are no longer logically capable of reproducing the effects associated with them in their traditional context. Pentheus is evidently the tragic hero of Euripides' play, but Soyinka's character of the same name is so radically altered that there is little prospect of his inspiring an audience to pity him or, indeed, to fear for themselves as they wonder what inscrutable fate might have in store for them. Unlike Euripides' Pentheus, who is driven by the desire to protect his kingdom from a vengeful cousin, Soyinka's character is a wholly paranoid tyrant who is obsessed with power and has no redeeming qualities whatsoever. As shown in the following excerpt, right from his first entry he projects the image of an overbearing authoritarian:

> I shall have order! Let the city know at once
> Pentheus is here to give order and sanity...
> I'm away only a moment
> Campaigning to secure our national
> frontiers. What happens? Behind me – chaos!
> The city in uproar. Let everyone
> Know I have returned to reimpose order.
> Order!

> (SCP 1, 256)

As is the case with the dictators in *A Play of Giants*, here the public space is so personalized that everything seems to be focused on the tyrant, or, at least, that is the way he sees it. Nevertheless, the contraction of all power into his hands alienates him from his grandfather, the former ruler, who feels totally excluded from the running of the state and who wishes that the young King gave him the opportunity to contribute his wealth of knowledge to the management of the kingdom. When Pentheus rudely accuses Tiresias, the seer, of having secretly joined Dionysos, the old King advises his grandson not to violate all the Theban rules of etiquette. Indeed, Tiresias himself is disgruntled with Pentheus' refusal to accord him the respect to which he is traditionally entitled. Thus Pentheus is not only tyrannical, but also undermines some of the most cherished values and traditions of the Thebans, suggesting that he is far from being the expected custodian of the ethical ideals of his people. He thus exhibits the tragic flaw of blindness to one's overweening pride that is common among protagonists of classical tragedy; the motives underlying his blindness, however, are not as pure as Creon's in Sophocles' *Antigone*, for example, but are patently expressive of petty-mindedness. Soyinka robs his Pentheus of the redeeming potential of tragic blindness, but instead presents him as wholly corrupt and, in a way, beyond the redemptive succour afforded by what the playwright himself would consider the truly wholesome tragic experience.

It is also noteworthy that, unlike Euripides' Pentheus, Soyinka's is also extremely sexist, as shown in the following excerpt:

> And tell it to the women especially, those
> Promiscuous bearers of this new disease.
> They leave their homes, desert their children
> Follow the new fashion and join the Bacchae
> Flee the hearth to mob the mountains.
>
> (*SCP 1* 256)

In his view, Dionysos' new religion undermines the traditional role of women; but what he fails to realize is that in fact the women, including his own mother, find in the Bacchic worship a form of autonomy hitherto undreamed of.

It is not only the women that find Pentheus totally oppressive and Dionysos liberating, but also those who are enslaved. Soyinka introduces the element of slavery to the play, substantially modifying the original. This addition has the effect of universalizing Pentheus' oppressive rule, for he is not only patriarchal, and a violator of cherished Theban values and practices, he is also a hard taskmaster and one who enjoys torturing the enslaved. Significantly, when the play opens Pentheus has just ordered an old slave to be ritualistically flogged as a way of cleansing the community's accumulated annual sins. The slave leader threatens a revolt if the old man dies, and, fearing the consequences of this and also on account of his own desire not only to be a witness to suffering, but also to be part of it, Tiresias offers to be flogged instead of the old slave. However, his gesture of solidarity does not stop the slaves longing for freedom from Pentheus' tyranny. Thus Dionysos becomes a welcome redeemer, as is made obvious by the slave leader's praise-song:

> For he is the living essence of whom, said heaven...
> Tribute to the holy hills of Ethiopia
> Caves of the unborn, and the dark ancestral
> spirits. Home of primal drums round which
> the dead and living
> Dance.

(SCP 1 248)

Clearly, Soyinka has brought into the metaphysical frame of the play a distinctly African cosmology, with the reference to Ethiopia partaking of its double signification as the realm of the orientalist image of Africa typical of classical and biblical representations as well as those common in eighteenth-century literature such as Samuel Johnson's *Rasselas*, and also as a symbol of uncolonized Africa institutionalized by its choice as the home of the Organization of African Unity. Besides, Soyinka alludes to the transatlantic slave trade, foregrounding the need to relate issues of culture and civilization to questions of the political economy of labour and justice.

On the whole, though, his main purpose for introducing the element of slavery is to universalize the constituency of the victims of Pentheus' despotism, showing that he has oppressed different sections and races of his nation, which makes the enthusiastic welcome Dionysos receives a genuinely communal and representative form of support for the new dispensation. Dionysos, then, is the archetypal Soyinkan liberator, embodying the anti-hegemonic spirit of the Atunda ideal as well as Ogun's fearless, but emancipatory transgression of oppressive alienation. It is also noteworthy that the paradigmatic interchangeability of Ogun and Dionysos in the domain of political agency is not the only thing they have in common: they are similarly partial to wine.

Furthermore, it may also be observed that it is a mark of Pentheus' evil nature that it is his own mother who tears him limb from limb, albeit under the Bacchic influence. In Euripides' play this is supposed to dramatize the barbarity of Bacchic worship; however, in Soyinka's text it is an extreme but understandable gesture of a radical dismemberment not of a son, but a monster of a tyrant. It is worth recalling the similarity between Agave's action and Isola's patricide in *Camwood on the Leaves*: both, tragically, have little choice but to defend themselves against a member of the family who has turned into a violent tormentor. Besides, the redemptive value of Agave's act lies in the fact that her transgression leads not only to the possibility of regenerating the whole society of Thebes, but the rehabilitation of Pentheus as well. In the final scene the severed head of Pentheus squirts red wine rather than blood, and the partaking of this wine becomes a sort of symbolic communion of reconciliation. This allusion to Christianity is, in fact, part of the play's abundant usage of biblical symbolism, within which Dionysos' agency and acts are framed within the terms of Christian redemption. The conceptualization of redemptive agency in Christian terms is common in African discourses of nationalism, and this is well illustrated in Ngugi wa Thiong'o's *A Grain of Wheat*, in which the whole language of Mau-Mau liberation is validated by biblical authority.[5] Indeed, unlike Euripides' Pentheus, Soyinka's is forgiven as he himself becomes the unwilling sacrifice required for the cleansing of the sins of Thebes.

It is also significant that, whereas Pentheus is the protagonist of Euripides' play, in Soyinka's version this role is taken by Dionysos. The inversion says a lot about Soyinka's prioritization of liberatory agency in his notion of tragedy, whereby the focus is not on the fate of those who, out of a combination of personality flaws and destiny have their fortunes reversed, as in the case of Euripides' Pentheus, but those who, like Dionysos, courageously confront tyranny and consequently free not only themselves but others as well. This is a significant reinterpretation of Classical tragedy and represents one of Soyinka's most important formal contributions to twentieth-century dramaturgy.

Whatever else the play achieves, one thing that is so glaringly different about it from Euripides' original is that Soyinka has made Dionysos not only the god of the Bacchantes and revellers, but also of would-be Atundas and Oguns. The idea of transformative tragedy is examined further in his sustainedly metaphysical play, *The Strong Breed* (1963). The play specially focuses on the way in which traditional African rituals of atonement are both paradigmatic and metonymic of the structure of tragedy in so far as tragedy itself serves as the paradigm of redemptive political agency.

The play is about Eman, a member of the strong breed, a group of carriers whose job involves annually dumping a boat symbolically loaded with all the accumulated evil of the year into the sea. However, Eman refuses to follow his father's footsteps after his girlfriend Omae dies, as is the case with all mothers of the strong breed, giving birth to their son. He takes up teaching in another part of the country where they have a different carrier tradition: they don't have designated carriers as in his village, but use a stranger or someone deformed. He prevents them from sacrificing the mute boy who plays about his house and instead offers himself as a carrier. He is killed, but the sacrifice of the village schoolteacher does not offer the sense of wholesomeness the community expects after such an event.

In the concept of tragedy at work in the play, the metaphysical and the mundane are not wholly inseparable, thus according with Soyinka's view that Yoruba gods are terrestrial and not removed from the site of human drama, just as humans are themselves capable of experiencing divine being, especially in the masquerades where they can even dress and assume the role of a given god.[6] Thus, for Soyinka, it is in tragedy that the duality of human ontology is most supremely re-enacted, offering an exploration of the divinity of the human, but a divinity that is not so much a case of displaying the splendour and power of supernatural alterity, but rather of revelling in the nobility of an individual's self-sacrifice offered in order that his community may be revitalized and transformed by his act and example. This relationship between the individual and society, according to Soyinka, is based on the fact that there is a 'visceral intertwining of each individual with the fate of the entire community' (*MLA* 53), making transformative agency simultaneously an individual as well as a communal act. Thus Eman becomes the quintessential Soyinkan tragic hero as he saves the mute boy from his death and offers himself as a substitute sacrifice. There are also some biblical echoes in the play, as in many ways Eman functions as a Christlike figure, occupying the same paradigmatic category as Soyinka's Dionysos and Ofeyi, for instance.

Nevertheless, in the concept of tragedy presented in *The Strong Breed*, as in *Season of Anomy* and *Death and the King's Horseman*, it is important that the tragic hero chooses his tragic action. We see Eman rejecting the ascriptive tradition of his village, where one is born into a role rather than willingly taking it up as an ethical and political choice. He tells his father, 'I am totally unfitted for your work father. I wish to say no more.' (*SCP 1*, 134) There are parallels here with the special role assigned to 'choice' within existentialism, a philosophical tradition with which Soyinka shows familiarity, particularly in its theatrical context. For most existentialists, the difference between an authentic and inauthentic being is marked by whether or not a subject has made a choice as to the nature of his/her life or existential project. In this respect, Eman's counter-identification with dominant ideology is not dissimilar to that of Albert Camus' hero in *The Outsider*. However, one should not stretch the resemblance between Soyinka's character and Camus' too far, since Camus' Meursault rejects dominant social values wholly for the sake of an individualist quest, whereas Eman does so because he wishes to return the practice of the carrier to its original redemptive capacity which has been lost through its routinization.

Once again, we see Soyinka presenting a tragic hero who is both the extension of his community and also its transformative alterity, emerging from the community, but standing apart in his function as its social and political possibility. It is a difference which is not conceived of in essentialist terms, but which is seen as a function, among others, of a determinate choice. Nevertheless, Soyinka makes the relationship between destiny and free will complicated, subtly suggesting that Eman's choice, in the final analysis, may itself be the inescapable call of his blood. Indeed, his father warns him that this might be the case: 'Your own blood will betray you son, because you cannot hold it back. If you make it do less than this, it will rush to your head and burst it open.' (*SCP 1*, 134) The idea of fate as determining the tragic hero's fortune shows Soyinka still working, albeit imaginatively, within the terms of Classical tragedy, but the overall context into which the concept is transplanted is radically different from the original. As he has argued, especially in his essay 'The Fourth Stage', there are parallels between some African and Greek cosmologies; however, such similitude does not make the two cultures reducible to each other, but provides an opportunity for the kind of comparative study of structural correspondences as well as differences that Soyinka undertakes both in his critical and creative work.[7] Thus, analysis of his usage of particular Western forms may be helpful in certain circumstances, but not generally, since in his creative and critical practice there is such an imperceptible blending of Western and African culture that the original identities of the constituent elements are irrecoverably erased and subordinated to the exploration of the role of the tragic in the provision of social and political plenitude.

The value of Eman's sacrifice is no less problematic. It is true that the community is renewed by his death, but the nature of that renewal is not very clear. If Eman's sacrifice had been intended to purge the community of the previous year's sins, this is evidently not the case, for most of the villagers are in shock at the display of their village teacher as a ritual sacrifice. The elders, Jaguna and Oroge, are confused that the sacrifice they have offered has not been received well by the people:

JAGUNA. ...We did it for them. It was all for their common good. What did it benefit me whether the man lived or died. But did you see them? One and all they looked up at the man and words died in their throats.
OROGE. It was no common sight.

(SCP 1, 146)

However, it is made clear in the text that Jaguna's reasons for choosing Eman are not as innocent as he claims, for he wants to get rid of him because Eman is going out with his daughter and he objects to his daughter's relationship with a foreigner. Thus the ritual merely serves as the convenient means of expelling a transgressive Otherness, making tradition an instrument of personal interest in a way reminiscent of the Kadiye in *The Swamp Dwellers* and the Baroka in *The Lion and the Jewel*. This, however, does not take away anything from the boldness of

Eman's decision to be the carrier, though it does, all the same, problematize it, making it a function of a variety of forces and desires rather than simply of an individual's Herculean act of willpower. In this, Soyinka seems to acknowledge the exceptional nature of the tragic hero while at the same time refraining from turning such distinctiveness into a possible source of narcissism on the part of the hero or hagiography on the part of the community, either of which would blunt the radical efficacy of the sacrifice and return it to the domain of the will to personal power that is the hallmark of dictatorship.

Even so, *The Strong Breed* does offer some regeneration to the community. It gives them a greater understanding of the transformative limitations of their ritual, which depends for its effectiveness on the demonization of foreigners: when the foreigner they are presented with is their own schoolteacher they come face-to-face with their collective inhumanity. It is evident that things will never be the same after Eman's death. Thus, in spite of the hybridity of the metaphysical conception of tragedy in the play, it remains one of Soyinka's most elaborate stagings of traditional African tragedy. For a complex hybrid text, though, we must turn to his *Death and the King's Horseman* (1976).

Based on a historical event that took place around 1946, the play offers one of the most intricate illustrations of Soyinka's notion of the tragic. His dramatic representation of the event is not the first, as there has been a Yoruba version and even a German film of it. The basic plot of the story is that, on the occasion referred to, a colonial English District Commissioner ordered the arrest of a Yoruba Oba who, as is customary, was preparing to commit suicide to accompany the King who had recently died.[8] When the Oba was arrested, his son took his father's place and committed ritual suicide, and thus the interruption of an age-long tradition had been avoided. Evidently, even by his own admission, Soyinka has expanded significantly on this original plot, and it is in the nature of that elaboration that his use of the play to develop his own idea of tragedy further becomes obvious. In Soyinka's version, on the evening of the Prince of Wales's visit to a colony, which is clearly Nigeria, Pilkings, a District Commissioner, orders the arrest of Oba Elesin, who is engaged in the same act as his historical counterpart. In a hurry to go to a masked ball, and regarding the

74

whole affair as an inconvenient barbarism, he locks up Elesin in his study, hoping to protect him by releasing him the following day, when his suicide would be unnecessary. Unbeknown to him, this touches on the most sensitive area of local belief and the community is about to riot when, in a moment of dramatic irony, he is saved by Olunde, Elesin's son, whom he himself has sponsored to study medicine in the United Kingdom.

Olunde causes his father and the whole community a lot of grief when he abdicates his traditional role of a King's horseman by going to England, but in the end it is he rather than his father who saves the community from the ignominy of an unfulfilled sacrifice. As Soyinka has pointed out, it is facile to reduce the play to the usual dichotomy of cultural conflict, as it is precisely such binary conceptions of the relationship between African and Western traditions within the totality of the African experience which the play interrogates. In its relentless examination of the import of that historic encounter between the two cultures, the play reveals not only the presence of cultural conflict, but also of different modes of the tragic. It is as a combination of the classical conception of the tragic and the traditional African form such as presented in *The Strong Breed* that the play explores the thematic significance of the actions of the two principal characters, Elesin and Olunde.

Elesin conforms fully to the Aristotelian notion of tragedy. Believing that he is destined to enact ritual suicide, an event that he has been prepared for since his youth, Elesin demands the best that his community has to offer before his departure, including the best food and a beautiful bride. However, as he is interrupted by Pilkings' intrusion, he makes an error of judgement, committing 'the unspeakable blasphemy of seeing the hand of the gods in this alien rupture of his world' (*SSP* 210). Even then, his failure to will himself to death completely is presented as a result of his weakness for worldly pleasures, and thus it is not only the interference of alterity that arrests Elesin's transition to the other world, but also his own tragic flaw. In the end he suffers the embarrassment of prison, but even more painful, of being scoffed at by his own people. Iyaloja, the leader of the market women who had sung him into the commencement of his tragic journey, becomes the vehicle of communal condemnation, telling him bluntly:

IYALOJA. You have betrayed us. We fed you sweetmeats such as we hoped awaited you on the other side. But you said No, I must eat the World's left-overs . . . No, you said, I am the hunter's dog and I shall eat the entrails of the game and the faeces of the hunter.

(*SSP* 211)

The Elesin's downfall could not be more complete: the King's horseman is now the coward imprisoned in Pilkings' library, and, to add insult to injury, he is treated to the spectacle of Pilkings, who has just come back from the Prince's masked ball and is completely oblivious to his transgression, speaking to him wearing the religious Egungun mask. Thus we have the typical instance of Aristotelian peripeteia or reversal in the fortunes of the hero.

However, in Olunde's substitution of himself for the father we have the deployment of Soyinka's concept of the redemptive potency of tragedy which is most supremely present in *The Strong Breed*. By becoming the agent of the renewal of his people's spirituality, Olunde confounds both tradition and modernity. Like Eman in *The Strong Breed*, he had revolted against being a carrier by duty rather than choice. His training as a doctor in England makes it even more unlikely that he will return to take up his hereditary role. On the contrary, that very experience has given Olunde a greater appreciation of his culture, which is conveyed with considerable authority as he explains to Pilkings the significance of the ritual suicide to his father, Elesin, and the community:

No one can understand what he does tonight without the deepest protection the mind can conceive. What can you offer him in place of his peace of mind, in place of the honour and veneration of his own people? What would you think of your Prince if he refused to accept the risk of losing his life on this voyage?

(*SSP* 194)

What is interesting here is that Olunde's access to Western culture has, in fact, erased the difference between it and his own, contrary to Pilkings's and his father's expectation. We are thus shown that the transgression of cultural boundaries may not necessarily lead to the transformation of a subject's fundamental beliefs and that, if anything, it may in fact entrench them more deeply. Moreover, the play foregrounds the arbitrariness of cultural valorization within the colonial formation, while also representing the scene of modernity as equally appropriate for training future Kings' horsemen. So when they bring the dead body of the King's horseman in the shape of the medic Olunde, something more than the traditional ritual has been performed, for the union between modernity and tradition that has been enacted here ensures that the practice is continued within the hybrid cultural formation of the post-colonial.

Thus, in the transgression of the difference between the modern and the traditional, Olunde not only regenerates a particular community at a determinate moment, but also opens up the colonial moment to the dialectic of transformation, metonymically staging a deeper form of cultural nationalism and anticipating the post-colonial critique of the uncritical valorization of tradition in nationalist discourses of identity. Thus here, as in the other texts we have examined in the chapter, Soyinka presents tragedy as that structure of symbolic resources in which change and renewal can be re-imagined endlessly.

5

Conclusion

In conclusion, it can be argued that Soyinka primarily works within the modes of both satire and tragedy, employing the former principally as the language of critique, of revealing the corrupt underbelly of the post-colonial malformation as well as its colonial antecedent, and the latter as the discursive site where political and social change are enacted as possibility, a restaging of the primal Ogunian traversing of the abyss of alienation and the Atunda will to counter-identification. However, in Soyinka's framework, these are merely strategies rather than irrevocably separate modalities of engaging with the hegemonic, for, as we have seen in those texts where the two modes are deployed together, satire and tragedy can be profitably combined to offer the most piercing gaze at the tragic banality of post-colonial power. Indeed, it is Soyinka's ability to work with antinomies while also interrogating their axiomatic premises, that makes his work challenging and also amenable to contemporary post-Marxist and post-Structuralist readings.

However relevant contemporary cultural theories are to the study of Soyinka's work, and by extension to other African writers too, one needs to ensure that the use of such critical discourse does not rob the writer's work of its cultural specificity and historical rootedness. Soyinka has always written in response to particular pressing issues of his society, where he simultaneously addresses the problems of Nigeria and those of other African countries as well as of the African diaspora. One would have to take into account the totality of his immediate ideological context in order to preserve the distinctiveness of his cultural project while also opening it up to other avenues of interpretation, a performance of the dynamic critical hybridity presupposed by the writer's own critical practice.

In this regard, his essays and the numerous interviews he has given, as well as his journalism, offer a useful resource for specifying his cultural location. They highlight some of the political issues and intellectual debates which inspired particular aspects of his creative and critical work. That is certainly the case with his first collection of essays, *Myth, Literature and the African World* (1976). On its publication, it was Soyinka's first book-length examination of the relationship between literature and culture in Africa. It is also a rigorous attempt to theorize and map out fundamental paradigms of African creative cultural practice in both European and indigenous languages. Moreover, it provides Soyinka with the opportunity to develop further his mythopoesis, as well as to illustrate its practical value as an analytical method for contemporary African literature. It is well known that his mythopoesis has given Soyinka an aesthetic, but what is never fully appreciated is that it has also provided him with a distinct mode of critical language which, in some important ways, resembles the symptomatic readings proposed by, for example, Pierre Macherey in his *A Theory of Literary Production* (1978). This is especially so in Soyinka's readings of ideologies underlying particular textualizations of the postcolonial, where he engages with the textual gaps and silences in a manner reminiscent of Macherey's critical practice. This is perhaps not the place for a detailed consideration of the relationship between certain modes of African criticism and contemporary cultural theory. Suffice to say that an appreciation of Soyinka's creative achievement that does not take into account his magisterial critical work such as *Myth, Literature and the African World* is incomplete, for his creative work, in so far as it shares the same metaphysical and conceptual foundation as his critical project, is another instance of critical elaboration, just as the converse is also true.

Soyinka's second collection, *Art, Dialogue and Outrage* (1988), contains useful essays, for example, on the relationship between the writer and the modern African state, as well as setting out his views on African Marxist literary criticism. It also features the essay in which he makes the famous attack on the authors of *Decolonising African Literature* (1985) who have unfairly depicted him as culturally alienated and also a tool of Western neo-colonial cultural Modernism. Soyinka's rejoinder is powerful for its passion, wit, sarcasm, and argumentative vigour. On the whole, the collection shows the writer engaging with a diversity of issues, most of which are examined in the context of his own location in Nigeria, especially the Nigerian academy, but without fail, his affiliation to the immediate is accompanied by a broadening of ethical and political concern and reference to matters affecting other parts of the continent as well as the world at large.

Another milestone in Soyinka's critical writing is his slim but significant essay *The Credo of Being and Nothingness* (1991), which is a theological treatise on the value of the much-maligned traditional African religion which is often stereotyped as, for example, witchcraft, black magic, sorcery, or voodoo. Soyinka attempts to codify the religion, even giving quotations from the holy book he came up with when his and his fellow-worshipper's attempts to get the University of Ife to give them a place of worship, as it had to Moslems and Christians, had been met by the argument that, since their faith did not have a holy book, it could not be treated equally with the established religions. In the usual way Soyinka deals with such matters, he set about composing a holy book himself, but prospective disciples will have to wait to have access to it, since it has not been fully published as yet.

Soyinka's theological concerns could be dismissed as a manifestation of his occasional eccentricity were it not that they are, in fact, an extension of his ideas on democracy and justice. His adoption of traditional African religion is based on the fact that, as it is not constitutively proselytizing, it obviates the need to go about enlisting members forcibly, which has historically been the case with Islam and Christianity in Africa, causing wars and other forms of conflict. Thus Soyinka has moved beyond using traditional belief for a mythopoesis and a political philosophy – he has come to embrace it as a personal faith. However, it is also clear that his conception of this faith is not just a matter of a metaphysical conception of the beyond, but very much of a template for engendering justice in the here and now, making his religious ideology closer to the liberation theology of Latin America than anything else. Perhaps there is always a conflict between the young Soyinka of the vicarage in Abeokuta and the Professor of Comparative Literature and

Theatre Studies who led a procession of a group which Christians would describe as 'animists', but members of which would most probably call themselves ancestral worshippers.

In 1996, while in exile, Soyinka published *The Open Sore of a Continent*, which, as indicated in the subtitle, is a personal narrative of the post-1980 political crisis in Nigeria, when a corrupt civilian government led by Shehu Shagari was replaced by a succession of military governments, the latest of which has actually scuppered the efforts to return the country to civilian rule. The book, which is essentially a distillation of previous public lectures, gives illuminating details on the embeddedness of corruption and violence in Nigeria; but, as usual, Soyinka does not allow himself to be so despondent that he cannot see the possibility of change. The resistance movement against Shell and the Federal Government of Nigeria by the people of Ogoniland led by the late Ken Saro Wiwa is one of the numerous examples he recounts of exceptional courage in the face of a brutalizing, vengeful and oppressive alliance of socio-economic and political forces.

As a political report on the state of the country, *The Open Sore of a Continent* extends the work begun in the writer's prison memoirs, *The Man Died* (1972), an account of Soyinka's imprisonment between 1967 and 1969, and it is also a text in which the writer seeks to unravel the nature of public power in his country by showing that the way the prison system was run and managed reflected the macrocosmic operations of power in the country. It is, however, as a record of the extremity of brutality that a post-colonial state can visit upon its citizens that Soyinka's memoirs demonstrate that the crisis of post-colonial leadership is less an abstract issue of management than an index of the profound erosion of the humane basis of politics. This is strongly illustrated by the fact that the title *The Man Died* actually registers the death of a helpless victim of post-colonial state violence. Equally, *The Open Sore of a Continent* starts with an account of another man who dies, Ken Saro Wiwa.

The gravity of Soyinka's political narrative is in marked contrast to his autobiographical writing, in which he is able to reconstruct his life and those of members of his family in a style that is abundantly humorous. In *Ake: The Years of Childhood* (1981) he gives his mother the nickname 'Wild Christian' and names his father 'Essay'. He also recalls his father, who was a school headmaster, insisting that a teacher who had plucked a rose from his garden return it to its stalk. After attempting to do so and failing, the teacher tries to impress on the Headmaster the impossibility of the task, but with little success until he enlists the help of Soyinka's mother. The story ends happily, with the teacher forgiven, but having learnt the lesson that one should not go around plucking other people's flowers without permission, especially if such persons also happen to be one's school headmaster. Generally, the biography expresses Soyinka's deep respect and love for his parents as well as for the whole extended family, which seems to have played an important role in his upbringing. Relevant to his career as a writer is the fact that he came from a background where literacy was taken for granted and where, as a child, he had access to books, which must have helped his educational and creative development.

There is also ample evidence that his later interest in politics must have been stimulated by the fact that a number of the adults around him were directly involved in all forms of anti-colonial resistance, including cultural nationalism. From the account, Soyinka seems to have observed from close quarters a significant event in the history of Nigeria, when the legendary Mrs Ransome-Kuti, mother of the late Jazz singer Fela Kuti and one of the early leaders of the modern Nigerian women's movement, led a group of women to protest against the colonial government's taxation of women. Soyinka's mother also took part in organizing the protest. In fact, she is herself part of the Ransome-Kuti family which has played an important role in the modern history and culture of Nigeria. So it would appear that Soyinka's interest in politics, indeed just as that of his much-lamented late cousin Fela, has also to do with coming from an environment in which it was not unusual for adults to stand up against oppressive authority, and in which they were themselves part of the modernizing class of the mission-educated élite. A number of the writers of Soyinka's generation, including Chinua Achebe, come from such a background.

What is significant in Soyinka's portrayal of this class of leaders is his emphasis on the degree to which they defined their role in ethical terms, albeit predominantly Christian ones, which enabled them to maintain links with the communities and cultures from which they had come, thus avoiding the sort of cultural alienation that afflicts members of a later generation of teachers, such as Lakunle of *The Lion and the Jewel*. So, the women's movement which had begun as a forum for discussing middle-class women's issues, for example, quickly transformed itself into a radical mass movement bringing together women from all social strata and also augmenting and extending further the anti-colonial movement.

The negotiation between tradition and modernity is very much the subject of *Isara: A Voyage around Essay* (1989), an imaginative reconstruction of his father's times before and during the Second World War. It is based on some documentary fragments Soyinka found in a metal tin after his father's death, and as such it is wholly a product of his imagination, making no claims to being a factually accurate biography, but rather the cross between fact and fiction known as 'faction'. This is the generic category in which Soyinka's most recent autobiography, *Ibadan: The Penke-lemes Years* (1994), is also located. He says, '*Ibadan* does not pretend to be anything but faction, that much-abused genre which attempts to fictionalize facts and events, the proportion of fact to fiction being totally at the discretion of the author' (p. ix). Among other things, the biography recounts Soyinka's post-Leeds experience, an Orwellian down-and-out period in Paris after being conned by an impresario who had been at his performance at the Royal Court in 1959. Mostly, it is about his return to Nigeria and his subsequent life, as an academic, a theatre director, and a political activist.

Taken together, the biographies reveal a life into which much diverse activity has been packed. Soyinka has been a night-club bouncer, teacher, builder, singer, tramp, professor, detainee, road marshall, journalist, and Nobel Laureate. His self-presentation is shaped to a significant extent by his literary imagination: so much so that in all his biographies there are numerous occasions when he departs considerably from the conventional patterns of biographical narrative, tending more and more towards fictional representation. This is particularly evident on the occasions when his love of the unusual makes him singularly highlight abnormally funny and tragic aspects of his life. Most memorable is the account given of the verbose inventor of the term 'Penkelemes', a malapropism for 'peculiar mess', in *Ibadan*. Soyinka tells us that when the politician was accused of embezzling funds, he drove his big American car to the marketplace and told the vendors that it was their car and they were free to ride in it or do whatever they wanted with it, and that that was where he had spent the money that had disappeared from the treasury. Obviously, all the vendors were behind him, singing his praises and carrying him shoulder-high. Side by side with such humorous episodes are some detailed accounts of degradation and violence, showing again the writer's ability to present human suffering together with his strong belief in its possible amelioration and total eradication.

It has been my concern here to contest the view sometimes cherished even by some of his admirers, that Soyinka is a difficult writer. Yes, he is, but he is accessible and extremely rewarding to read. One of the reasons for this is his knack of seeing things from an unexpected point of view, in order to provide a fresh perspective on the conventional and familiar. His is quintessentially a poetics of defamiliarization, employing satire and tragic comedy as well as tragedy itself as discursive sites from which to engender a renewed awareness of the nature of post-colonial reality in its full historical and continuing encounter with other cultures, particularly and significantly those of the West.

Notes

CHAPTER 1. INTRODUCTION

1. See James Gibbs, *Soyinka* (London, 1986).
2. James Gibbs, ' "A Storyteller on the Gbohun-Gbohun": An Analysis of Wole Soyinka's Three Johnny Stories', in James Gibbs and Bernth Lindfors (eds), *Research on Wole Soyinka* (Trenton, NJ, 1993), 37–47.
3. Soyinka, 'The Critic and Society: Barthes, Leftocracy and other Mythologies', in Henry Louis Gates, *Black Literature and Literary Theory* (London, 1990).
4. Odia Ofeimun, 'Kole Omotoso', *Perspectives on Nigerian Literature: 1700 to the Present*, 2 (Lagos, 1988), 185.
5. Soyinka, *The Credo of Being* (Ibadan, 1991), 17.
6. See Jacques Derrida, *Of Grammatology*, trans. Gayatri Chakravorty Spivak (London, 1976); Homi Bhabha, *The Location of Culture* (London, 1994).
7. Edward Said, *Orientalism* (London, 1978); Abdul R. JanMohamed, *Manichean Aesthetics* (Amherst, 1983).
8. For example, Femi Osofisan, 'Wole Soyinka and a Living Dramatist', Adewale Maja-Pearce, *Wole Soyinka: An Appraisal* (London, 1994), 43–60.

CHAPTER 2. SATIRICAL REVELATIONS

1. Bernth Lindfors, 'Soyinka', in Leonard Klein *et al.* (eds), *African Literatures in the 20th Century* (London, 1988), 136–7.
2. Dapo Adelugba, *Before Our Own Eyes* (Ibadan, 1987).
3. James Gibbs, ' "A Storyteller on the Gbohun-Gbohun": An Analysis of Wole Soyinka's Three Johnny Stories', in James Gibbs and Bernth Lindfors (eds), *Research on Wole Soyinka* (Trenton, NJ, 1993), 38.

4. Ibid.
5. For some discussion of missionaries and local-language literature see Gareth Griffiths, 'Writing and Literacy', and Mpalive Msiska, 'East and Central African Writing', in Msiska and Hyland (eds), *Writing and Africa* (London, 1997).
6. Ibid.
7. Soyinka's reply to such critics in an interview-preface with Biodun Jeyifo in the Methuen collection.
8. James Gibbs, *Talking with Paper: Wole Soyinka at the University of Leeds 1954–1958* (Powis, 1995).
9. 'Telephone Conversation', in Gerald Moore and Ulli Beier (eds), *Modern Poetry from Africa* (Harmondsworth, 1963), 111–12.
10. See Gibbs, *Talking with Paper*.
11. Mary Louise Pratt, *Imperial Eyes: Travel Writing and Transculturation* (London, 1992).
12. The term 'symbolic arbitrary' is used in the manner employed in Pierre Bourdieu and Jean-Claude Passeron, *Reproduction in Education, Society and Culture* (London, 1977).
13. Robert July, 'The Artist's Credo: the Political Philosophy of Wole Soyinka', *Journal of Modern African Studies*, 19/3 (1981), 477–98.
14. Preface to *A Play of Giants*, p. x.
15. Ngugi wa Thiong'o, *Homecoming* (London, 1972).

CHAPTER 3.   TRAGIC COMEDIES AND COMIC TRAGEDIES

1. See Femi Abodunrin, *Blackness: Culture, Ideology and Discourse* (Bayreuth, 1986), 92; and Mark Kinkead-Weekes, '*The Interpreters: A* Form of Criticism', in James Gibbs (ed.), *Critical Perspectives on Wole Soyinka* (London, 1981), 229.
2. See James Gibbs, *Wole Soyinka* (London, 1986).
3. James Gibbs, *Talking with Paper: Wole Soyinka at the University of Leeds 1954–1958* (Powis, 1995).
4. 'Been-too' is a person who has been abroad.
5. Louis Althusser, *Lenin and Philosophy, and other Essays* (London, 1971).
6. See Derek Walcott, *The Antilles: Fragments of Epic Memory: The Nobel Lecture* (London, 1993).
7. Brenda Cooper, 'The Two-Faced Ogun: Post-Colonial Intellectuals and the Positioning of Wole Soyinka', *English in Africa*, 22/2 (October, 1995), 44–69.
8. For a concise description of the masquerades, see Gibbs, *Wole Soyinka*.

CHAPTER 4. REDEMPTIVE TRAGEDIES

1. See Biyi Bendele-Thomas, 'Soyinka Interviewed', in Adewale Maja-Pearce (ed.), *Wole Soyinka: An Appraisal* (London, 1994), 142–60.
2. Eldred Durosimi Jones, *The Writing of Wole Soyinka* (London, 1973), 27.
3. Jones, *The Writing of Wole Soyinka*, 201–2.
4. This concept of agency is developed further in my 'Geopoetics: Subterraneanity and Subversion in Malawian Poetry', in Abdulrazak Gurnah (ed.), *Essays on African Writing* 2 (London, 1995), 73–99.
5. Ngugi wa Thiong'o, *A Grain of Wheat* (London, 1965).
6. See Soyinka, *Myth, Literature and the African World* (1976), 10–19. Ibid, 145.
7. Ibid, 140–60.
8. For some general information on the historical aspects of the play, see James Gibbs, *Wole Soyinka* (London, 1986).

Select Bibliography

AUTHOR'S WORK

Creative Writing

Plays

Soyinka Collected Plays 1: (Oxford: Oxford University Press, 1973). Includes *A Dance of the Forests, The Swamp Dwellers, The Strong Breed, The Road* and *The Bacchae of Euripides*.

Soyinka Collected Plays 2: (Oxford: Oxford University Press, 1974). Includes *The Lion and the Jewel, Kongi's Harvest, The Trials of Brother Jero, Jero's Metamorphosis,* and *Madmen and Specialists*.

Soyinka: Six Plays (London: Methuen, 1984). Includes the Jero Plays, *Camwood on the Leaves, Death and the King's Horseman, Madmen and Specialists* and *Opera Wonyosi*.

Other Published Plays

A Play of Giants (London: Methuen, 1984).

Requiem for a Futurologist (London: Rex Collings, 1984).

Childe Internationale (Ibadan: Fountain Press, 1987).

From Zia, with Love and *A Scourge of Hyacinths* (London: Methuen, 1992).

The Beatification of Area Boy: A Lagosian Kaleidoscope (London: Methuen, 1995).

Poetry

Idanre and Other Poems (London: Methuen, 1967).

A Shuttle in the Crypt (London: Rex Collings, 1972).

Ogun Abibiman (a long poem) (London: Rex Collings, 1976).

Mandela's Earth and Other Poems (London: Methuen, 1989).

Novels

The Interpreters (London: Andre Deutsch, 1965).

Season of Anomy (London: Rex Collings, 1973).

Autobiography, Memoirs, Translations
The Forest of a Thousand Demons (London: Nelson, 1968) (translation of D.
    O. Fagunwa's novel, *Ogboju Ode Ninu Igbo Irunmale*).
The Man Died: Prison Notes (London: Rex Collings, 1972).
Ake: The Years of Childhood (London: Rex Collings, 1981).
Isara: A Voyage around Essay (London: Methuen, 1989).
Ibadan: The Penkelemes Years – A Memoir, 1946–1965 (London: Methuen,
    1994).

Interviews
Duerden, Dennis and Cosmo Pieterse (eds), *African Writers Talking* (New
    York: Africana Publishing House, 1972).
Gates, Henry Louis, 'Interview with Prof. Wole Soyinka', *Black World*, 24/
    10 (1975), 30–48.
Borreca, Art, 'An Interview with Soyinka: Idi Amin was the Supreme
    Actor', *Theatre*, 16/2 (Spring, 1985), 32–7.
Bendele-Thomas, 'Biyi, Interviewed: 3 July, 1993, Notting Hill Gate', in
    Adewale Maja-Pearce (ed.), *Wole Soyinka: An Appraisal* (London:
    Heinemann, 1994), 133–41.

Criticism, Essays, Addresses
Myth, Literature and the African World (Cambridge: Cambridge University
    Press, 1976).
'We Africans must Speak in One Tongue', *Afrika*, 20/9 (1979), 22–3.
The Critic and Society: Barthes, Leftocracy and Other Mythologies (Ife: Ife
    University Press, 1981).
'Theatre in African Traditional Culture: Survival Patterns', in Onlani-
    yan, Richard (ed.), *African History and Culture* (Ikeja: Longman
    Nigeria, 1982), 237–49.
'Shakespeare and the Living Dramatist', *Annual Survey of Shakespeare
    Studies and Production* (Cambridge: Cambridge University Press,
    1983), 1–10.
Art, Dialogue and Outrage (essays) (Ibadan: New Horn, 1988).
'Jihad for Freedom', Index on Censorship, 18/5 (1989), 20–1 and 30.
'Twice-Bitten: The Fate of Africa's Cultural Producers', *PMLA* 105/1
    (Jan., 1990), 110–20.
'Spiking the Wall: A Lecture' (London: The Institute of Contemporary
    Arts, 1990).
The Credo of Being and Nothingness (Ibadan: Spectrum Books and Jersey,
    Channel Islands: Safari Books Export, 1991).
'Nobel Prize Lecture, 1986: The Past Must Address its Present', Maja-

Pearce, Adewale (ed.), *Wole Soyinka: An Appraisal* (Oxford: Heinemann, 1994), 1–21.

The Open Sore of a Continent: A Personal Narrative of the Nigerian Crisis (Oxford: Oxford University Press, 1996).

SECONDARY SOURCES

Biographical

Adelugba, Dapo (ed.), *Before Our Very Eyes: Tribute to Wole Soyinka* (Ibadan: Spectrum Books, 1987).

Gibbs, James, 'Bio-Bibliography: Wole Soyinka', *African Library Journal*, 3 (1972), 15–22.

—— 'Date-line on Soyinka', *New Theatre Magazine*, 12/ 2 (1972), 12–14.

—— *Talking with Paper: Wole Soyinka at the University of Leeds, 1954–1958* (Powis: Nolisment, 1995).

Jahn, Janheinz, Ulla Schild, and Almut Nordmann, *Who is Who in African Literature: Biographies, Works, Commentaries* (Tübingen: Horst Erdmann, 1972).

Lindfors, Bernth, *Black African Literature in English: A Guide to Information Sources, 1936–1976* (London: Hans Zell, 1989).

—— *Black African Literature in English, 1977–81* (London: Hans Zell, 1985).

—— *Black African Literature in English, 1982–1986* (London: Hans Zell, 1989).

Zell, Hans, Caroline Bundy, and Virginia Coulon (eds.), *A New Reader's Guide to African Literature* (London: Heinemann, 1983).

Critical Studies

Abodunrin, Femi, *Blackness, Culture, Ideology and Discourse* (Bayreuth: Eckhard Breitinger, 1996).

Achebe, Chinua, 'The Novelist as a Teacher', in Msiska, Mpalive-Hangson and Paul Hyland (eds), *Writing and Africa* (London: Longman, 1997), 278–81.

Althusser, Louis, *Lenin and Philosophy and Other Essays* (London: New Left Review, 1971).

Amuta, Chidi, 'From Myth to Ideology: The Socio-political Content of Soyinka's War Writings', *The Journal of Commonwealth Literature*, 23/1 (1988), 116–29.

Appiah, Kwame Anthony, 'Myth, Literature and the African World', Maja-Pearce, Adewale (ed.), *Wole Soyinka: An Appraisal* (Oxford: Heinemann Educational Publishers, 1994), 98–115.

Arnold, A. James, *The Poetry and Poetics of Aime Cesaire* (Cambridge,

Mass.: Harvard University Press, 1981).

Balogun, F. Odun, 'Wole Soyinka and the Literary Aesthetic of African Socialism', *Black American Literature Forum*, 22/3 (Fall, 1988), 503–30.

Bhabha, Homi, *The Location of Culture* (London: Routledge, 1994).

Bourdieu, Pierre and Jean-Claude Passeron, *Reproduction in Education, Society and Culture* (London: Sage, 1990).

Boyce-Davies, Carole, 'Maidens, Mistresses, and Matrons: Feminine Images in Selected Soyinka Works', Carole Boyce-Davies and Anne Graves (eds), *Ngambika: Studies of Women in African Literature* (Trenton, NJ: Africa World Press, 1986), 75–88.

Chinweizu, Onwuchekwa Jemie and Ihechukwu Madubuike, *Toward the Decolonisation of African Literature* (London: Kegan Paul International, 1985).

Cooper, Brenda, 'The Two-Faced Ogun: Post-Colonial Intellectuals and the Positioning of Wole Soyinka', *English in Africa*, 22/2 (October, 1995), 44–69.

David, Mary T., *Wole Soyinka: A Quest for Renewal* (Madras: B. I. Publications, 1995).

Derrida, Jacques, *Spectres of Marx* (London: Routledge, 1994).

Fanon, Frantz, *The Wretched of the Earth* (London: Penguin, 1967).

—— *Black Skin, White Masks* (London: Pluto Press, 1991).

Feuser, Willfried, 'Soyinka: The Problem of Authenticity', *Black American Literature Forum*, 22/3 (Fall, 1988), 555–75.

Gates, Henry Louis, 'Introduction', *Black American Literature Forum*, 22/3 (Fall and Winter, 1988), 3, 4.

Gibbs, James (ed.), *Wole Soyinka: Critical Perspectives* (London: Heinemann, 1980).

—— *Wole Soyinka* (London: Macmillan, 1986).

—— Ketu Katrak, and Henry Louis Gates, *Wole Soyinka: A Bibliography of Primary and Secondary Sources* (Westport, CT: Greenwood Press, 1986).

—— and Bernth Lindfors, *Research on Wole Soyinka* (Trenton, NJ: Africa World Press, 1993).

Gillespie, I. S., 'No Need for Tigritude: The Holy Anger of Wole Soyinka', *Encounter*, 74/2 (March, 1990), 48–51.

Griffiths, Gareth and David Moody, 'Of Marx and Missionaries: Soyinka and the Survival of Universalism in Post-Colonial Literary Theory', *Kunapipi*, 11/1 (1989), 74–85.

Gurnah, Abdulrazak (ed.), *Essays on African Writing Vol. I* (London: Heinemann, 1993).

Gurr, Andrew, 'Third World Drama', in James Gibbs (ed.), *Wole Soyinka: Critical Perspectives* (London: Heinemann, 1980), 139–46.

Hand, Sean (ed.), *The Levinas Reader* (Oxford: Blackwell, 1989).

JanMohamed, Abdul R., *Manichean Aesthetics: The Politics of Literature in Colonial Africa* (Amherst: University of Massachusetts, 1983).

Jeyifo, Biodun, 'Tragedy, History, and Ideology', in Georg Gugelberger (ed.), *Marxism and African Literature* (Trenton, NJ: Africa World Press, 1986), 94–109.

Jones, Eldred Durosimi, *The Writing of Wole Soyinka* (London: James Currey and Heinemann, 1973).

Ketrak, Ketu-H., *Wole Soyinka and Modern Tragedy* (London: Greenwood Press, 1986).

Kinkead-Weekes, Mark, '*The Interpreters*: A Form of Criticism', in James Gibbs (ed.), *Critical Perspectives on Wole Soyinka* (London: Heinemann, 1981).

Lindfors, Bernth, 'Beating the White Man at his own Game', *Black American Literature Forum*, 22/3 (Fall, 1988), 475–88.

Macebuh, Stanley, 'Poetics and the Mythic Imagination', in James Gibbs (ed.), *Wole Soyinka: Critical Perspectives* (London: Heinemann, 1980), 200–12.

Matejka, L. *et al.* (eds), *Readings in Russian Poetics* (Cambridge, Massachusetts: MIT Press, 1971).

Mbembe, Achilles, 'The Banality of Power in the Post-Colony', *Public Culture*, 4/2 (Spring, 1992), 1–30.

Moore, Gerald, *Wole Soyinka* (London and Ibadan: Evans Brothers, 1978).

Msiska, Mpalive-Hangson and Paul Hyland (eds), *Writing and Africa* (London: Longman, 1997).

Ngugi wa Thiong'o, *Homecoming* (London: Heinemann, 1972).

Nkosi, Lewis, *Tasks and Masks* (London: Longman, 1981).

Obiechina, Emmanuel, *An African Popular Literature* (Cambridge: Cambridge University Press, 1973).

Ogunba, Oyin, *The Movement of Transition: A Study of the Plays of Wole Soyinka* (Ibadan: Ibadan University Press, 1975).

Ojaide, Tanure, 'Two Worlds: Influences on the Poetry of Wole Soyinka', *Black American Literature Forum*, 22/4 (Winter, 1988), 767–76.

Omotoso, Kole, *Achebe or Soyinka? A Reinterpretation and a Study in Contrasts* (Oxford: Hans Zell, 1993).

Osofisan, Femi, 'Wole Soyinka and a Living Dramatist', in Adewale Maja-Pearce (ed.), *Wole Soyinka: An Appraisal* (Oxford: Heinemann, 1994), 43–60.

Pieterse, Cosmo and Donald Munro (eds), *Protest and Conflict in African Literature* (London: Heinemann, 1969).

Quayson, Ato, *Strategic Transformations in Nigerian Writing* (Oxford: James Currey, 1998).

Roscoe, Adrian, *Mother is Gold: A Study in Western African Literature* (Cambridge: Cambridge University Press, 1971).

Said, Edward, *Orientalism* (London: Routledge, 1978).

Senkoro, Fikeni E. M., *The Prostitute in African Literature* (Dar es Salaam

Publishing House, 1982).

Straton, Florence, *Contemporary African Literature and the Politics of Gender* (London: Routledge, 1994).

Taylor, Patrick, *Narrative of Liberation: Perspectives on Afro-Caribbean Literature, Popular Culture, and Politics* (Ithaca and London: Cornell University Press, 1989).

Wauthier, Claude, *The Literature and Thought of Modern Africa* (London: Heinemann, 1978).

Wright, Derek, *Wole Soyinka Revisited* (New York: Twyne, 1993).

Young, Robert, *White Mythologies: Writing History and the West* (London: Routledge, 1994).

Index